Macs on the Go!

Guide to Mobile Computing

For Mac laptops using Mac OS X

John Tollett with **Robin Williams**

Peachpit Press
Berkeley · California

Macs on the Go

John Tollett with Robin Williams

Copyright ©2006 by John Tollett and Robin Williams
Cover design: John Tollett
Cover image of the earth from iStockPhoto.com
Interior design and production: John Tollett and Robin Williams
Index: Emily Glossbrenner

Peachpit Press

1249 Eighth Street
Berkeley, California 94710
800.283.9444
510.524.2178 phone
510.524.2221 fax

Find us on the web at **www.peachpit.com**

To report errors, please send a note to **errata@peachpit.com**

Peachpit Press is a division of Pearson Education

ISBN 0-321-24748-5

10   9   8   7   6   5   4   3   2   1

Printed and bound in the United States of America

Dedicated to the ones we love

To Josh, Scarlett, Jimmy, and Ryan. For treasured memories, journeys, and adventures together— both digital and otherwise. In a computerized world of amazing connections, you're the best, the most reliable, and the most enjoyable.

Many Thanks

A big Road Warrior "thank you" to Ross Carter, a true
Renaissance Man, for generously sharing technical
knowledge that helped us to better understand and
explain some of the geeky stuff. To quote Shakespeare,
"You are the man."

Thanks, Mike McGurl, for sharing your Mac tech-support
expertise with us, for being generous with your time, and
for joining us for breakfast and Mac-conversations when
we run into you at Harry's Roadhouse. (Insider Road
Warrior tip: check out Harry's Roadhouse if you're in
Santa Fe, New Mexico.)

Lots of thanks and love to Pat Williams (Robin's Mom)
for being our tester of everything from video chats around
the world to podcasts on Web pages. Pat is one of a rare
brand of senior citizen who gives her old computers and
Mac tech-support to her children.

Special thanks to Nancy Davis and David Van Ness at
Peachpit for including a whopping amount of patience
and kindness in their skill sets.

Many thanks and lots of gratitude to iStockPhoto.com
for being there with a fabulous collection of stock images
that's easy to search and affordable to use. The globe image
on the cover and the web site is from their collection.

Finally, thanks to readers who send in Road Warrior
tips, photos, or stories of on-the-go adventures for the
book's companion web site. Visit **web.mac.com/roadrat**
for details.

Contents

9 Wi-Fi and Hotspots
A Wireless Primer
163

10 File Sharing
On the Go
175

Extra
Road Warrior Tips 195

Introduction

As Robin and I prepared for a recent trip to the Mid-East, we decided to "travel light." We packed just enough clothes to get by, plus a gadget bag filled with a Palm handheld PDA, a small video camera, 30 blank mini-DV tapes, a digital still camera, and two gigabytes worth of Compact-Flash cards—plus an assortment of adapters and battery chargers. Oh yeah, and a Garmin GPS. We decided to leave the laptop at home (the "travel light" thing). After all, we had a Wi-Fi PDA with us, Internet cafes are everywhere, and many of the hotels we'd be staying in would surely provide computers and connections for their guests.

This "travel light" concept seemed to be working great the first couple of days. In New York, as we waited for our flight to Egypt, I used my Wi-Fi–enabled Palm to send a short email to the .Mac Group Page we created just for the trip. It was awkward typing on the teeny little keyboard, but it was fun being so mobile and "light." "Road Warriors must sometimes be willing to endure hardships like this," I said as I retyped the same sentence five times and watched the battery drain on the Palm Tungsten C handheld device.

A couple of days later in Alexandria, using my PDA, I detected an open Wi-Fi network on the balcony of our room overlooking the Mediterranean Sea. Cool. I sent a short update to our .Mac Group Page (too tired to deal with typing a long message on a teeny little keyboard, or trying to get the portable, folding, infrared keyboard to work). By now, the PDA needed charging. I used an adapter to plug the PDA charger/cradle into the wall plug. Oops—forgot to check the voltage on the back of the charger before we left; this was the only electronic device in our pack that needed a transformer. The PDA is OK, but the charger is toast. OK, no problem—Plan B—use PCs in Internet cafes and hotels.

This Alexandrian cafe had water pipes, but no Wi-Fi.

Plan B worked, but not as well as traveling with our own laptop. Ooh, how easy and fun it would've been to download and organize my photos every night while relaxing in the hotel room, instead of having a thousand hi-res photos to download and organize after I got home. And how convenient it would have been to write updates for the .Mac Group Page while lounging in bed, then send them whenever a connection was available. And, as you may know, using Windows on a hotel's PC is not the elegant experience that we Mac users expect from a computer.

As for Internet cafes, they were more scarce in Egypt and Jordan than in places like Pokhara, Nepal, and our daily schedule was so packed with adventures and discoveries, we just didn't have enough free time available to find them. I wondered, could someone back home FedEx my laptop to me? Is there an Apple Store in Luxor? Do they take American Express? No, no, and yes.

The next time we "travel light," it'll be because I've replaced most of those heavy clothes items with a Mac laptop (and maybe a transformer). But I don't expect to have any trouble next time because we just wrote this book and it contains all the information needed for successful mobile computing, plus lots of tips that'll make even new laptop users feel like seasoned Road Warriors.

This book was written for laptops with Mac OS X Tiger installed, but a great deal of the information also works just fine for Mac laptops that use older versions of Mac OS X (Jaguar and Panther).

Gotta run! My new EVDO card arrived!

Being Mobile
Things You Can Do

For those of us who own a laptop computer, such as the iBook or PowerBook, *to be or not to be mobile* is not really the question. Even if the extent of your travels is only to carry your laptop from one side of the house to the other, you're mobile. So, for most of us, the question actually is "How mobile do I want to be?"

Depending on your needs and what services or accessories you're willing to buy, the answer to this question can range anywhere from "I want to check my email from the bedroom" to "I want to be a Road Warrior."

How many ways can a person be mobile? More than we can cover in this book. Our information centers primarily around your laptop and how to use it with a minimum of extra gadgets and paid services. However, some of and services are very useful, so we'll cover quite of few of them.

Robin connects via Wi-Fi on the steps of a closed Starbucks in London—across the street from Shakespeare's Globe Theatre.

A Bluetooth-enabled mobile phone can talk to your Bluetooth-enabled laptop. If your mobile plan includes Internet service, you can let your mobile phone act as a modem and connect your laptop to the Internet.

This Garmin GPS device saved a lot of wrong turns as we traveled through England's countryside.

A Palm PDA with built-in Wi-Fi is one of our favorite gadgets when we don't want to carry a laptop to the nearest Wi-Fi hotspot.

An EVDO PC card and service can provide a wireless broadband connection almost anywhere.

How Mobile Do You Want To Be?

The easiest answer to this question is "Whatever my laptop can do." That's quite a lot and should make you feel happily connected. For a while. When you eventually start lusting for more mobile capability, you may have to invest in some extra peripherals and accessories, but you'll still have *most* of what you need right there on your Mac laptop.

So, as a Road Warrior, what are some of the mobile capabilities you can expect from your Mac laptop?

Home and office mobility

▼ **Your laptop as the ultimate portable office.** Mobility isn't always about connecting to the Internet or to other computers. Sometimes it's just about having all your applications and files with you, bundled up onto a nifty little computer so you can get work done while on the go—anything from writing a letter to editing a movie. It's like having your entire office available to you at all times.

If you want a change of scenery, just pick up your laptop and move to another desk or another room. Or find a comfortable recliner and put your laptop on your lap.

▼ **Connect to the Internet wirelessly.** If your laptop has a wireless card, you can jump on the Internet anywhere that's within range of an existing wireless network. That could be in your office hallway, on your bedroom patio, or sitting on the front steps of a building in Luxor that has a Wi-Fi connection.

▼ **Entertain yourself.** While traveling, you can listen to your music collection from iTunes, listen to an audio book, or watch a movie on dvd. When a Wi-Fi connection is available in an airport, the wait for a flight goes by very quickly because you can access the iTunes Music Store to preview or buy single songs, albums, audio books, and even videos and some television programs.

▼ **Read your RSS feeds.** If you've set up RSS feeds for information you're interested in, you'll get the feeds anywhere in the world—once you're connected. You won't have to miss out on anything.

▼ **Download and listen.** If you've subscribed to some favorite podcasts, you can collect and listen to them while on the road. Don't miss a single episode!

▼ **Professional presentations.** Like many business people, we often give presentations to groups of people. A laptop enables you to create a presentation while on the go—or make last-minute revisions.

If your audience is small, you don't even need a projector—just present straight from your computer.

▼ **Video conferencing and chatting.** Since Wi-Fi connections are broadband and fast enough to support video chats, you can use iChat and an iSight camera (or any FireWire video camera) to video conference from any Wi-Fi hotspot—a hotel room or lobby, a coffee shop, or an airport that provides wireless access. If you don't have a FireWire video camera, you can use your laptop's built-in microphone to audio chat, or just use text chat with family members, buddies, or business associates who are online.

The Apple iSight camera's small size and light weight make it easy to pack and travel with. Some of the newest laptops have iSight cameras built into the frames.

Up to four people can video chat at a time, but it requires a very fast broadband connection and a very fast Mac.

Two-person video chats are mostly trouble-free and have reasonably good video quality.

Hosting additional video participants may noticeably degrade the quality of the video, depending on your Mac.

▼ **Download and read.** All major newspapers and magazines are available in digital form. Some are free and others require a paid subscription. You can click on a topic in the table of contents and immediately jump to that article; click on a web address in an ad and jump directly to the advertisers web site.

Some digital publications are viewable on the web and others need special reader software, such as Zinio Reader. The example below shows *Macworld* magazine as it appears in the Zinio Reader on my PowerBook.

When I click on the edge of a page, the page turns with a realistic animation. Since the magazine has been downloaded to my PowerBook, I can read it anytime, anywhere—even without an Internet connection.

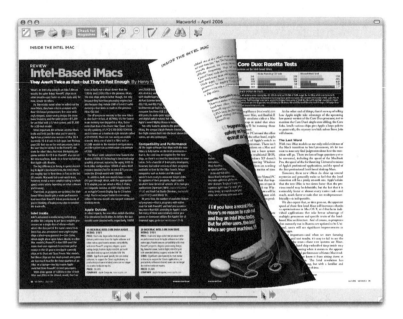

The Zinio Reader provides a real-world magazine experience, complete with page-turning animation.

▼ **Use your laptop with other portable devices.** A Mac laptop can be used with a Bluetooth-enabled mobile phone, a Palm PDA, and the most popular GPS devices. In Chapter 11 we talk about how this can be useful and offer how-to information, tips, and resources for more information.

▼ **Take advantage of .Mac convenience.** If you have a .Mac account (pronounced "dot Mac"), your Road Warrior challenges are easier in many ways. You can use .Mac Mail, a web mail feature that's accessible from any computer anywhere in the world. You can use the .Mac HomePage feature to almost instantly create and publish photo albums, newsletters, or résumés online. When you need to get a very large file or a folder full of photos to someone, you can create an FTP (File Transfer Protocol) page such as the one shown below, upload the files to your .Mac iDisk storage space, password-protect the FTP page if you want, then send the page address and password to the person who needs access. They can go to your .Mac FTP page and download the files at their convenience. The very cool mobility advantages of having a .Mac account are covered in Chapter 4.

During the research, writing, design, and production of this book, I used my .Mac account as a place to put files so my editor could download them when it was convenient. In this example, I've uploaded a PDF file of the book's cover design to a password-protected .Mac FTP site.

There's no way for my boss to know I was actually in Hawaii instead of my office in Santa Fe, New Mexico.

▾ **Synchronize and access vital information.** Being a mobile computer user allows you to carry around your important personal information, such as your Address Book contacts, appointments in iCal, and your custom collection of Safari (Apple's web browser) bookmarks.

Use iSync and your .Mac account to synchronize your personal information with a duplicate copy on your .Mac iDisk (the personal storage space on Apple's computers that's included with a .Mac account). You can then synchronize that copy of your information with another computer. For instance, if you're on the go and away from your office, someone in your office can update your calendar or contacts, then you can sync the updated information to your laptop from anywhere an Internet connection is available. See Chapter 4 for more about iSync.

▼ **Do even more.** Some very interesting things are made possible by certain services. Some cost money, others are free. For instance, you can call someone's telephone and talk to them from your computer. Learn more cool ways to be mobile and productive in Chapter 11.

▼ **It's not just about you.** We've discovered that one of the most appreciated hospitalities you can offer house guests is a wireless Internet connection and the use of a laptop computer during their stay. Guests can take the laptop to their room, check their email, or take care of business. If they brought their own laptop, they might be excessively grateful for the connection. If you don't have a wireless network set up in your home or office, it's probably because you don't realize how easy

A guide to information in this book

There is so much information in this book that it will probably be hard to absorb everything. Below is a quick reference to specific things you might want to know, organized so you can find it easily.

There are **three things you really should have** to travel most effectively with your Mac: **a wireless card** (which is built into all Mac laptops today), **a .Mac account** (see Chapter 4), and the software package from Apple called **iLife '06** (or later; it includes iPhoto, iWeb, and four other applications).

Photographs

iWeb and HomePage sites or pages can be password-protected. Also see the information about file sharing in Chapter 10.

▼ **Share your photos publicly**
- .Mac slides: Any Mac OS X user can subscribe to your slideshow of photos; they appear as a screen saver. See page 87.
- iWeb photos page. Any computer user can view your photos on a web page. See pages 88–95.
- .Mac HomePage. Upload photos for any computer user to view. See pages 182–186.

▼ **Share your photos privately**
- Photocast. Mac users of your choice download an iPhoto album of yours into their own iPhoto applications. See page 96–97.
- .Mac Group page. Invited members, using any computer, can all share photos with each other. See pages 82–85.

Accessories

▾ Hardware

- Some "essentials" are listed on pages 13–19.
- Security devices are on pages 148–149.
- Need a device to help you find wireless networks? See page 167.
- If you need an external modem, see pages 11 or 159.
- If you have to use a modem, some accessories you may find handy are on pages 162 and 218.
- A little bit of information on iPods, GPSs, and PDAs is on pages 214–215.

▾ Software

- Troubleshooting software. See page 198.
- Widgets useful for traveling. See pages 166, 199–200, and 213.
- Online maps. See pages 201–209.
- Broadband Tuner for better connectivity. See page 215.
- .Mac account. See Chapter 4.
- iLife '06. See the Apple Store at **www.Apple.com/store**. iLife is usually loaded on new Macs.

Communication

▾ Email

- .Mac web mail. See pages 71–74.
- Check your POP accounts. See page 71.
- Dial-up numbers around the world. See pages 159–160.
- SMTP account when on the go. See pages 72 and 156–158.

▾ Text chats

- Text message with iChat over the Internet. See page 101–108.
- Text message with other chat clients over the Internet. See page 210.
- Text message with others on your local network, using Bonjour. See pages 101 and 114–116.

▾ Audio chats

- With iChat over the Internet. See pages 101–105 and 109.
- VoIP (Voice over Internet Protocol) with Skype or Vonage. See page 211.
- Voicemail to your email box. See page 210.

▾ Video conferencing with up to four people

- Use iChat over the Internet. See pages 3, 101–105, and 110–111.

— continued

Modems, if you have to use one while traveling

- Network configurations for a modem. See pages 26–28 and 34–38.
- Internet Connect settings for. See pages 39 and 44–46.
- External modem, if you need one. See pages 11 or 159.
- Dial-up tips. See pages 159–162.
- Make a location for your settings for easy access. See pages 54–56.
- Extend your dial-up wirelessly with an Airport Station. See page 170.

Keep track of yourself, and let others know what you're doing

- Use iCal; publish your calendar so others can subscribe to it. See Chapter 6.
- Create a Groups page. See pages 82–85.
- Take advantage of travel widgets, and tell your friends at home about them. See pages 166, 199–200, and 213.
- Post a blog in iWeb. See pages 88–89.

Share your files with others around the world

- See Chapter 10.

Access your data when not at your own computer

- Use your iDisk. See pages 59–64.
- Get your Address Book contacts on any computer. See pages 75–77.
- Use your own Safari bookmarks. See pages 78–81.
- Access your iCal calendar; use iSync. See pages 65–70.
- Check your mail on any computer. See pages 71–74.
- Check your mail from another POP account. See page 71.

Get connected

▼ Ethernet Internet connection (broadband)
- See the Network settings on pages 26–28 and 30.
- Make a location for quickly changing settings. See pages 54–56.

▼ AirPort Express Base Station for wireless access
- See the Network settings on pages 26–28 and 32–33.
- Check the Internet Connect settings. See pages 40–43.
- Make a location for quickly changing settings. See pages 54–56.
- Take advantage of your wireless AirPort network. See pages 169–173.

▼ Bluetooth Internet connection
- See the Network settings on pages 26–28 and 31.
- Check the Internet Connect settings. See pages 47–49.
- Make a location for quickly changing settings. See pages 54–56.

Essential Hardware
for Mobile Computing

Most people assume that being mobile means lugging a laptop around with you. That's usually true, but not always the case. We sometimes travel without a laptop, assuming we'll be able to find Internet cafes along the way, or we may take along a Wi-Fi–enabled PDA or a mobile phone that can connect to the Internet. But nothing beats the convenience and versatility of having a small, portable computer with you that's loaded with your own music, photos, work files, applications, and settings.

To be truly mobile *and* productive, the one essential piece of hardware you need is a laptop. You may already have one, but just in case you're still shopping around, we'll quickly review the Mac laptop options. Then we'll look at some other hardware and accessories you might consider adding to your travel gear.

At the end of this chapter you'll find out how to access all the hidden secrets of your laptop keyboard.

Which Laptop to Buy?

Apple offers three laptops—*iBook G4*, *PowerBook G4*, and *MacBook Pro*. All current models already have **AirPort Extreme** installed, a wireless (Wi-Fi) card that can connect to a wireless network in your home, office, at many coffee shops and book stores, many hotels, and at thousands of other *hotspot* locations around the world.

Below is information about the current models of Mac laptops. Keep in mind that the models Apple offers change regularly!

*A **hotspot** is a location that provides wireless network access, usually for a fee and sometimes for free. See Chapter 9 for more information about hotspots and Wi-Fi.*

The iBook

The iBook is a consumer-level laptop (ideal for students) with a rugged and durable plastic case. You can get a 12-inch display for the ultimate in light-weight portability, or a 14-inch display for more screen real estate.

The 14-inch iBooks offer you a choice of either a *ComboDrive* or a *Super-Drive*. A ComboDrive can *read and write* (burn) CDs. It can also *read* a DVD (meaning that it can read the data on a data DVD, and it can play a movie DVD disc). But it can't *write* a DVD as a data disc or as a movie DVD. A SuperDrive, on the other hand, can do all of these things—read *and* write CDs *and* DVDs.

The screen quality may be a deciding factor in which laptop you choose if you plan to use it to edit photographic images or to give presentations to small groups without a projector. The contrast in an iBook screen can vary a lot, depending on the angle from which you view it. If you want to adjust colors or retouch image files, you have to make sure you have the screen at just the right angle to give you an accurate rendering of how the image really looks. If people are gathered around your laptop for a small presentation, the screen will look good to those directly in front, but it will be sub-par for everyone else.

The PowerBook

Apple's newest PowerBooks are aluminum-cased, professional-level laptops. They're slightly more powerful, they have more ports for plugging in other devices, and they offer up to a 17-inch display. A 17-inch screen makes the PowerBook's high-end model attractive to professionals and is increasingly replacing the desktop computer in the office. The PowerBook also has a higher-quality screen than the iBook, and higher resolution. These may not be critical considerations when you're traveling, but if you want your laptop to be your main (or only) computer when you're *not* on the go, give the PowerBook extra points for providing more options.

Like the iBook, PowerBooks also come with either a ComboDrive or a Super-Drive. If you choose the ComboDrive (which doesn't burn DVDs), you'll save a couple hundred dollars. Now, you may *think* you'll never have any reason to burn a DVD, just as Robin's mother and some of our friends thought. But it wasn't long before *they* were shooting digital photos, editing movies, and asking why we let them buy a computer without a SuperDrive!

If you can afford the extra expense, get the SuperDrive. Even if you aren't interested in making your own movies on DVD, and even if you don't need to back up data to a disc that holds more than four gigabytes, it'll probably be easier to sell your laptop later if it has a SuperDrive in it.

A PowerBook includes a PC card slot, also known among old-timers as a PCMCIA (Personal Computer Memory Card International Association) card slot. The PC slot accepts PC cards that can add different kinds of functionality to your laptop. Some PC cards, for instance, provide extra USB or Ethernet ports. Other PC card adapters hold digital media cards like the one your digital camera uses.

You can also buy a Microdrive—a miniature hard drive—and a PC card adapter (shown on the right) to add a gigabyte of removeable storage space to your laptop. Insert it into the PC card slot.

For presenters, some of the PowerBook models have back-lit keyboards that can sense when the ambient light is low and illuminate the keys, which enables you to see your keyboard in a dark presentation room. The built-in speakers on the PowerBook are more powerful and sound better than iBook speakers (of course, external speakers are much better for presentations; see page 18 for suggestions).

The MacBook Pro

The MacBook Pro is the first model of Mac laptops to feature Intel processors, boasting increased speed and performance. All of the Mac applications that are bundled with these new laptops have been specially optimized for the Intel chip. Many of your favorite third-party applications have been, or are in the process of being, optimized for this new processor. The biggest difference you'll notice—other than blazing speed—is the iSight camera that's built into the border of the screen.

An internal modem is *not* included in MacBook Pro laptops. If you need one, a tiny USB modem is available at the online Apple Store.

The PC card slot (described above) in a MacBook Pro uses a new and different technology, which means your old cards won't fit in it. The new slot is called an ExpressCard/34.

Robin's mom, Pat Williams, heading towards 80 years old, may be one of the only great-grandmothers in the world who hands off her old Macs to her children. When Pat got a new G5 with the Intel processor (she wanted to go wireless so she could get AirTunes, plus she wanted a SuperDrive so she could burn her movies), she gave her G4 iMac to Robin's brother, Cliff.

Microdrive card and adapter.

Apple USB modem.

Laptop Conclusions

The iBook is more affordable and it's durable—a nice feature for travelers, students, and other rugged types. It's a good choice if you want to be mobile *and* save a few dollars.

The PowerBook is a little more expensive (exactly how much more depends on the configuration you choose), but the extra speed, power, and higher-quality screen can be worth the extra money if you use the laptop as your primary work computer.

The MacBook Pro is the top-of-the-line laptop. Other models with the Intel processor will be available soon (probably by the time you read this).

Essential Mobile Accessories

While your Mac laptop and its included software will get you connected and online in most situations, there are some mobile accessories that make mobile computing, both domestic and foreign, easier and less stressful.

One small reality check: If you carry all this gear around with you, it means you're pretty much obsessed with this Road Warrior stuff. Your load can be lightened considerably if you eliminate the digital camera equipment from the list (which I personally consider more important than the convenience of traveling light).

Laptop carrying case

A nice carrying case helps protect your computer and gives you a place to keep most of your accessories together. I prefer a backpack-style computer bag because I usually also carry a camera bag that's large enough to hold a digital video camera and a digital still camera. When I wear the backpack, I still have one hand free to use my mobile phone, my PDA, my GPS, or my iPod. Or to show my ID to airport security agents.

Mini mouse

A laptop provides a trackpad, so you don't have to use a mouse. But for some of us, a mouse is much easier to use and the trackpad feels awkward. A mini mouse is extra small, lightweight, and packs away nicely. The small footprint of a mini mouse gives more room to maneuver when you're working in a crowded space, such as a cafe table or an airline fold-down tray.

A Targus mini mouse.

Search the Internet for "mini mouse" to find a wide selection of both wired and wireless (Bluetooth) models. Some of our favorites can be found at Targus. com and iogear.com. Don't forget to put a mouse pad in your bag.

Spare cables and cable adapters

It's better to take cables with you and not use them than to need a simple little cable and have to spend hours in an unfamiliar city trying to find one.

An RJ-11 cable.

▼ **Telephone cord (RJ-11).** This is an ordinary telephone cord to connect your laptop to a phone outlet so you can use your Mac's internal modem* to connect to the Internet. Sure, you hope your hotel has a broadband connection, but if it doesn't, you're prepared.

Also consider taking along a duplex adapter (shown to the right). Plug the adapter into a phone outlet, then plug both the phone and your laptop modem into the duplex end of the adapter. You can only use

A duplex adapter.

one device at a time, but you won't have to plug and unplug a phone cord every time you switch between making a phone call and going online.

*The MacBook Pro does not come with a modem installed unless you specifically request and pay extra for it.

▼ **Ethernet cable (RJ-45).** This is a very handy item to have in your laptop bag. Sometimes an Internet access area (a hotel business office, a resort community room, or an Internet cafe) provides an Ethernet port so you can connect to their broadband connection, but they might not provide the Ethernet cable you need to connect your laptop. Hotels that provide broadband connections in their rooms will often have an Ethernet port close to the telephone (sometimes labled as a "data port") that you can plug your laptop into using an Ethernet cable.

If you're at a client's office and need to transfer files between computers, you can use an Ethernet cable to connect two computers and share files. See Chapter 10 for more information about file sharing.

If you plan to use an AirPort Express to make your hotel room wireless, you'll need an Ethernet cable (see page 17).

▼ **FireWire cables.** A FireWire cable will connect most digital video cameras to your laptop. With your videocam connected, you can import video from your camcorder, then use iMovie to create a movie while you're on the go. I often use iMovie because it's so easy; with the click of a button I can create a streaming QuickTime movie and upload it to a web page on my .Mac account (see Chapter 4).

If you don't want to import video, you can connect the camcorder to your laptop and show your video on the laptop screen. We pack along two different FireWire cables so we can do this—a *4-pin to 6-pin* cable that connects a videocam to a computer, and a *6-pin to 6-pin* cable in case we want to connect to a FireWire portable storage device. Decide which cables you might need and take them with you.

FYI: The most common Ethernet cables are UTP-CAT5 (Unshielded Twisted Pair-Category 5). They can be *straight through* or *crossover.*

Straight through cables connect your computer to another device, such as a hub, a switch, or a wireless base station such as the AirPort Extreme Base Station.

Crossover cables connect two similar devices, such as two computers, two hubs, two routers, or a hub and a switch.

FYI: FireWire 400 devices and cables support transfer rates of 400 Mbps (megabits per second). FireWire 800 devices and cables are twice as fast (800 Mbps).

4-pin.   *6-pin.*

Some FireWire 400 cables have 6-pin connectors on each end.

Others, such as the cables used to connect digital video cameras to a computer, have a 6-pin connector on one end and a 4-pin on the other end.

FireWire 800 cables have 9-pin connectors.

▼ **USB cables.** Most devices that use a USB connection, such as iPod cradles, Palm device hot sync cradles, or digital media card readers, usually come with their own USB cables. Don't forget to pack them.

Power supplies

▼ **Battery chargers and batteries.** Some of the devices you might want to carry with you, such as a digital video camera, use rechargeable batteries and have their own dedicated battery chargers. Other devices, such as a Palm PDA, have built-in rechargeable batteries and a recharging cradle. These items are bulky and heavy, but if you're going to be on the go for more than a few days, it's easier to pack them than it is to do without them. We usually carry an extra package or two of AA and AAA disposable batteries for things like a wireless mic setup for our video camera or a handheld GPS unit.

▼ **An extra battery.** The online Apple Store sells batteries for Mac laptops. Traveling with an extra battery provides insurance that you can do what you need to do between battery charges or until you can connect to a power outlet. I also carry a couple of extra batteries for the video camera because they're harder to find than regular batteries (AA or AAA, etc.) that I may need. When I leave the hotel room, I usually leave one camcorder battery in the room, being charged, put one in the camcorder, and carry an extra, fully charged battery with me. Common sense, I know, but it's amazing how many times I've ignored my own advice and regretted it.

▼ **Plug adapters.** Electronic devices in North America use a 110/120V (volt) electric current; other countries use a 220/240V current. Mac laptops are dual-voltage, so you can plug them in anywhere, any country—*if* you have an adapter to make your power plug fit the shape of the power outlet in the wall because power outlets in other countries come in a variety of sizes and shapes. Before you leave home, buy a plug adapter that's compatible with the country you plan to visit. Electric adapter plugs for various countries are usually sold in travel and luggage stores or electronics stores.

Or visit LaptopTravel.com, TeleAdapt.com, TravelOasis.com, or iGo.com to find adapter plugs for different countries. They also have *global* electric adapter and surge protectors that fit most socket styles around the world.

You may also want to buy a **combo AC/DC power adapter.** It lets you not only power your laptop from a standard wall outlet, but also has

Tip: If you use an iPod, you can maximize its play time (up to 30+ hours) by getting one of the iPod battery packs that are available from third-party companies:

> *myPower* from Tekkeon (www.Tekkeon.com)
>
> *The iPod Battery* by Battery Technology (www.BatteryTech.com)
>
> *TunePower* from Belkin (www.Belkin.com)

Or search the web for "iPod battery pack."

Power adapters let you plug your computer or other device into a foreign power outlet.

Adapters DO NOT transform or convert the power supply—they merely help the American two-prong plug adapt to fit the foreign socket.

Tip: Search the web to find "electric adapter plugs." Or use one of these shopping sites to find the best price among dozens of online stores:

www.Shopper.cnet.com

www.PriceGrabber.com

www.BizRate.com

A transformer plugs into a power outlet (you may need an adapter!), then you plug your device into the transformer.

adapters to fit a car, your yacht, or an airplane power outlet. You'll find this type of multi-use adapter online at www.Kensington.com, as well as at many other online stores.

▼ **Power transformers.** As mentioned previously, your Mac laptop is designed to work with the power supply in other countries (once you can plug it in with a plug adapter). Make sure your other devices (such as battery chargers) are safe to plug into foreign wall sockets: Look on the back of the device to see if it's labeled for dual-voltage use.

If it says "100–240V," it is designed for dual-voltage use. You do *not* need a transformer.

If it says "110V," it's designed for use only in North America and you'll need a power transformer to safely plug it in elsewhere.

Many electronics stores, online and otherwise, sell power transformers. Transformers are bulky and heavy, but it's easier to pack one than to spend time trying to find one in an unfamiliar city.

The "Input" information on the back of this battery charger indicates it can work with electrical systems that use between 100 and 240 volts (anywhere in the world).

If the input value is "120" only, you need a transformer. If you plug the device into a wall running 240V without a transformer, you'll destroy the device.

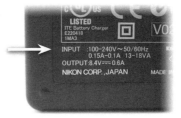

Do NOT use an external transformer with a Mac laptop because your power cable has a built-in transformer. If you add another transformer, the laptop will ignore the external power supply completely and run on battery power. Thus if you leave your laptop on thinking the battery is being charged because it's plugged into a power supply, you'll discover it is actually draining the battery.

*Don't forget to also pack a small **surge protector**! You can plug it into the wall with an adapter, and then have several outlets for your devices.*

Note! A **converter** is not the same as a **transformer**. A converter is what you need for *electrical* (as opposed to electronic) devices that have motors, such as hair dryers, shavers, irons, etc. A converter is meant for short-term use. And it is really heavy to carry around (it can be just as cheap to buy a hair dryer or iron in the country in which you'll be traveling—and it will weigh less).

Electronic devices like your computer, camera, etc., use transformers, not converters.

AirPort Extreme Base Station

The AirPort Extreme Base Station is not a portable device, but it does make you and your laptop more portable around the home or office. "Extreme" means the device is using the 802.11**g** wireless standard, which is five times faster than the 802.11**b** standard used in the original AirPort Base Stations. The 802.11**g** wireless networks are backward-compatible with 802.11**b** wireless devices, such as the original AirPort wireless cards, meaning they will work just fine with older devices.

To create a wireless Internet connection in your home or office, buy an Air-Port Extreme Base Station. Connect your phone line or broadband connection to it with an Ethernet cable. If your laptop has an AirPort Extreme Card installed, you'll be able to connect to the Internet wirelessly as long as you're in range, approximately 150 feet from the base station. If you have an older AirPort card installed in your laptop, it will still work but you'll be limited to transfer speeds of 11 Mbps.

AirPort Express Base Station

This device is not essential, but it can add a huge convenience to your mobile life. The AirPort Express is actually a small, portable base station that connects to an existing Internet connection and sends out a wireless signal. You can use it in two ways: to create a *new* wireless network, or to *extend* an existing wireless network. Both are explained on the following page.

To create a *new* wireless network: Plug the AirPort Express into a power outlet. Use an Ethernet cable to connect it to your broadband source (a cable or DSL modem) in your home or office or to the broadband data port (an Ethernet port) in your hotel room. Now your laptop can connect wirelessly to the Internet from anywhere in the room.

To extend the range of an *existing* wireless network: Plug the AirPort Express into a power outlet that's within range of the existing network.

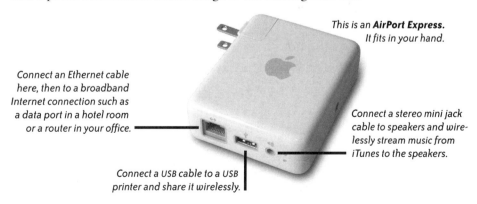

This is an **AirPort Express.**
It fits in your hand.

Connect an Ethernet cable here, then to a broadband Internet connection such as a data port in a hotel room or a router in your office.

Connect a stereo mini jack cable to speakers and wirelessly stream music from iTunes to the speakers.

Connect a USB cable to a USB printer and share it wirelessly.

Portable speakers

This is certainly something you can leave behind if you want to travel light, but if you have a presentation to give that includes audio, a set of powerful, portable speakers can make a giant difference in the audio quality and impact of the presentation. If you just want to play some songs from your iTunes music collection for a group of friends or show iMovies to relatives, portable speakers enhance the show. Or if you'll be spending a lot of time in that hotel room, bring your speakers; add an AirPort Express (previous page) and stream your music from iTunes to the speakers across the room or have stereo sound for your DVD movie.

Just a few of the nifty portable speakers worth checking out are:

- ▼ Altec Lansing inMotion Portable Speakers
  (www.AltecLansing.com)
- ▼ Creative TravelSound Portable Speakers
  (www.Creative.com)
- ▼ JBL On Tour Speaker System
  (www.JBL.com)
- ▼ JVC Mini Speakers
  (www.JVC.com)

Also visit the online Apple Store (http://store.apple.com) to see some of the latest portable speakers: On the Apple Store web page, select "Speakers" from the "iPod Accessories" category, which is (at the moment) on the left side of the web page.

The same portable speakers for your laptop will usually connect to an iPod as well, so you can share your iPod music collection with a large group or a small crowd. Or entertain yourself.

The Altec Lansing inMotion Portable Speakers can be used with or without an iPod (shown docked in middle).

Portable storage devices

If you plan to do a lot of work while on the go, or if you need to carry more files than your laptop will hold, external portable storage drives are the answer. They're available in all sizes and capacities from many brand-name suppliers. Although you can carry full-sized drives around with you, it's much easier to travel with a miniature drive that's designed for portability. The miniature drives are not only smaller and lighter, they usually don't require their own power supply.

Search the web or one of the many online shopping sites, such as PriceGrabber. com, for "mini drives." You'll find:

Micro mini drive. This thumbnail-sized drive usually has a USB 2 connection (faster than USB 1.1). Plug it into your USB port.

Mini drives. This drive is about half the size of a stick of gum. It usually has a USB 2 connection (faster than USB 1.1) Mini-drive capacities range from less than 1GB (gigabyte) to 100 GB.

Pocket drive. The pocket-sized drives come in both USB 2 and FireWire versions. Sometimes one drive includes ports for both.

In the past we often avoided editing movies during travel simply because digital video requires so much storage space on our laptop. Now we carry a 100 GB pocket drive so we can store imported video externally. In addition, a pocket drive is a fast and convenient backup solution. And it's an easy way to transfer files to someone else's computer. Just connect it to a FireWire-enabled computer and its icon appears on the Desktop.

An **iPod** can also be used as an external hard disk to store and transport files. Connect your iPod. In the iPod preferences in iTunes, check the box to "Enable disk use." Double-click the iPod icon on the Desktop. Drag files or a folder of files from any location on your computer to the iPod window that opens.

Tip: Keep a small pack of blank CDs in your laptop case so you can burn backups of important new files. CDs make it easy to share files with someone else.

The SmartDisk FireLite pocket drive.

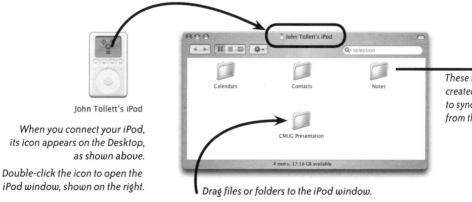

John Tollett's iPod

When you connect your iPod, its icon appears on the Desktop, as shown above.

Double-click the icon to open the iPod window, shown on the right.

Drag files or folders to the iPod window.

These three folders were created when I used iSync to synchronize contact info from the laptop to the iPod.

Laptop Keyboards Are Different

The keyboard on your laptop is slightly different from a stand-alone keyboard that comes with a desktop computer. The most obvious difference is that it's smaller and doesn't include a separate numeric keypad. But your laptop keyboard has lots of hidden secrets, most of which you'll access using the *fn* key.

The Function key

The *fn* on that key in the lower-left stands for "function." When you *hold down* the fn key, the normal function of certain keys (including some of the Fkeys) changes. For instance, the keys outlined below double as a numeric keypad. This *embedded* numeric keypad replaces the *dedicated* numeric keypad of a desktop keyboard.

iBook keyboard.

Hold down the function key to activate the embedded numeric keypad.

Tip: Instead of holding down the fn key, you can tap the "num lock" key (F6) to activate the numeric keypad.

Tap F6 again to turn off the keypad.

The small letters, numbers, or symbols in the bottom-right corner of some keys indicates how the functions of those keys will change when you hold down the fn key. For instance, the small "c" shown on the 6 key represents the "clear" command; it becomes available when you press the fn key to activate the numeric keypad.

People who use calculators or spreadsheets will find this feature especially valuable.

15- and 17-inch PowerBook keyboard.

A 17-inch PowerBook keyboard is shown above. Unlike the iBook keyboard, the F7, F8, F9, and F10 keys have default actions assigned to them, indicated by icons on the keys.

The F7 key shows an icon of overlapping rectangles. The rectangles represent computer screens. If you've connected your laptop to an external display such as another monitor or a projector, use the F7 key to toggle between *dual display mode* (your laptop display is extended to the connected external display) and *video mirroring mode* (whatever you see on your laptop is duplicated on the connected external screen, television, or projector).

Some PowerBooks have back-lit keyboards that sense the amount of ambient light. When light conditions in a room are too dim to see the keyboard characters, the PowerBook can illuminate the characters—a nice feature when you have to give a presentation in a darkened room.

The F8 key turns the keyboard illumination feature on or off.

Tap the F9 key to reduce the amount of illumination; each tap dims the keyboard more.

Tap the F10 key to increase the keyboard's illumination; each tap increases the light.

— continued

When you tap the F8 key, it's the same as clicking this checkbox in the Keyboard & Mouse preferences.

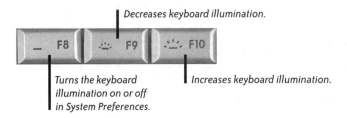

Decreases keyboard illumination.

Turns the keyboard
illumination on or off
in System Preferences.

Increases keyboard illumination.

If you try these Fkeys (shown above and explained on the previous page) and nothing happens, it may be that your Keyboard preferences are set so that the **fn key** is required to activate the default Fkey commands. Try pressing the fn key (circled below) along with the Fkey. See the next page for details about changing Fkey behavior.

Amazingly, the 12-inch PowerBook's keyboard (below) is the same size as the keyboard on the 17-inch PowerBook. But since the 12-inch PowerBook doesn't include a back-lit keyboard illumination feature, the F8–F10 keys don't show illumination control icons.

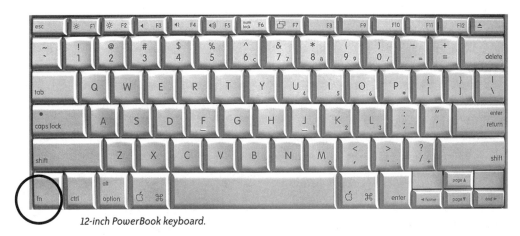

12-inch PowerBook keyboard.

Change the Fkey behavior

Many different applications use the Fkeys as keyboard shortcuts. For instance, in Adobe InDesign, I can press F5 to display or hide the Swatches palette and F6 to display or hide the Color palette. But when I work in InDesign on my PowerBook, when I press F5 it raises the sound volume instead of bringing up the Swatches palette.

You can change the Keyboard preferences so the Fkeys will perform the custom actions in other *software* applications instead of the default *hardware* actions assigned to them by the Mac.

1. Open System Preferences.

2. Click the "Keyboard & Mouse" icon.

3. In the "Keyboard & Mouse" window, click the "Keyboard" tab (circled below).

4. The Keyboard pane contains a checkbox to change the Fkey behavior.

    When the checkbox IS checked: The Fkeys will perform *software* features (custom actions that you've assigned in other applications).

    > If you want to use the F1–F12 keys to control *hardware* features (the features indicated by the icons on the keys) while this box is checked, press the fn key along with the appropriate Fkey.

    When the checkbox IS NOT checked: The Fkeys control *hardware* features—the features indicated by the icons on the keys (such as screen brightness and volume).

    > If you want to use the F1–F12 keys to perform *software* features (custom actions that you've assigned in other applications) while this box is checked, press the fn key along with the appropriate Fkey.

If this checkbox is selected, press the fn key along with one of the Fkeys to control hardware features such as volume, screen brightness, or keyboard illumination.

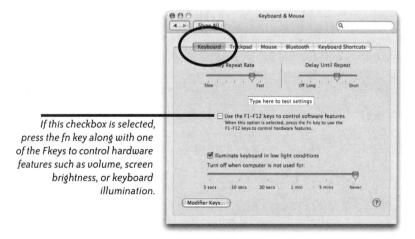

More fn functions

The keyboard chart below shows how key functions change when using the fn key, and the Fkey checkbox is *not* selected in Keyboard preferences (as explained on the previous page).

Press the fn key to make the Fkeys perform commands assigned to them in other applications.

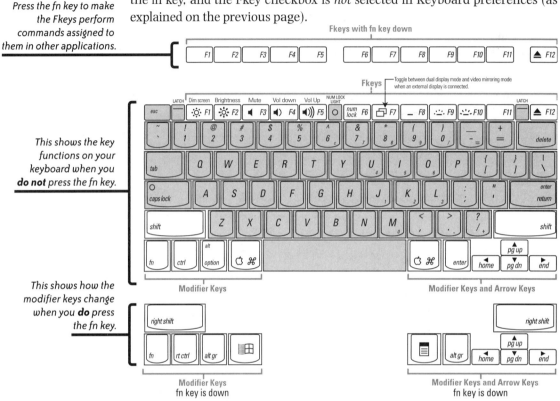

*This shows the key functions on your keyboard when you **do not** press the fn key.*

*This shows how the modifier keys change when you **do** press the fn key.*

Hold down the **fn** key and tap the Delete key to **forward delete.**

The **arrow keys** on the bottom-right turn into Home, PageUp (pg up), Page-Down (pg dn), and End when you hold down the **fn** key.

When you hold down the fn key, the Control key becomes the **Right Control** key (rt ctrl), and the Shift keys become **Right Shift** keys, which are necessary in some games where the right-side keys can have different features from the left-side keys. The Option keys become **Alt GR** keys, a CTRL-ALT combination for foreign characters.

The Windows key icon.

The Windows Menu Key icon.

The **Option, Command,** and **Enter keys** take on the functions of a *PC keyboard* when you hold down the **fn** key. This is useful if you're running Windows emulation software, such as Microsoft Virtual PC for Mac, that lets your Mac run Windows. The Command key becomes the **Windows key** that brings up the Windows Start menu. The Enter key becomes the **Windows Menu key** that accesses the right-button menus (like the Mac's contextual menus). And the Option key becomes an official **Windows Alt key.**

Network Preferences
for Mobile Computing

Since Mac laptops are designed to be mobile, everything you really need is already installed. Mobility doesn't always mean going places where you need a passport—moving your laptop between home and office, or between home office and bedroom, might be as mobile as you need to be.

In this chapter we'll explain a number of features to make sure you can get connected wherever you go.

We'll show you how to modify the various **Network settings** in System Preferences for different connection *ports* that you may need to use—Ethernet, AirPort, internal modem, FireWire, and Bluetooth. Use these settings to check the status of your connectivity, turn network methods on or off, and customize the preferences for various connection methods. See pages 26–38.

We'll also show you how to use **Internet Connect** to adjust the options and settings for AirPort, internal modem, and Bluetooth connections. See pages 39–53.

And we'll show you how to set up customized **Locations** so you can change the connection method and settings for various locations where you most often work (home, school, office, Internet cafe, satellite office, another country) with the click of your mouse. See pages 54–56.

The settings you will need to check most often as you connect around the world is the Network Status pane. Be sure to read pages 26–28 and become very familiar with turning port configurations on and off, prioritizing them, and checking the status of your connections!

Your Network Settings

Your Mac laptop can connect to the Internet in several different ways. It depends on the type of Internet connection available and whether or not your laptop has Bluetooth or AirPort installed.

To open your Network settings, click the System Preferences icon in the Dock (below-left). Then click the "Network" icon (below-right).

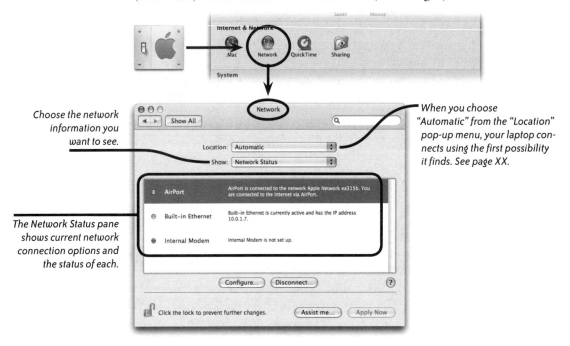

Choose the network information you want to see.

When you choose "Automatic" from the "Location" pop-up menu, your laptop connects using the first possibility it finds. See page XX.

The Network Status pane shows current network connection options and the status of each.

The Network Status pane

To see the current connection possibilities, from the "Show" pop-up menu, make sure "Network Status" is selected (it probably is). The possible connections you might see in the Network Status pane are listed below. If your laptop doesn't have Bluetooth or AirPort installed, you won't see those options.

▼ **Built-in Ethernet.** You can use an Ethernet cable to connect your laptop to a broadband connection, such as a DSL or cable modem. You can also use an Ethernet cable to connect to the Ethernet port of a wireless base station, such as Apple's AirPort Base Station. See page 29.

▼ **AirPort.** If your laptop has an AirPort card installed, you can wirelessly connect to an Apple AirPort Base Station. You can also connect to any wireless access point that transmits a Wi-Fi signal (Wi-Fi hotspots are available at many locations around the world). See pages 30–31.

- ▾ **Internal Modem.** The internal modem port uses an ordinary telephone cable (RJ-11) to connect to a phone outlet. Internal modems are not capable of fast speeds, but they're a lot faster than no connection at all. (If you want to send a fax, you have to use the internal modem and connect a phone line, even if you have access to a broadband connection.) See pages 32–35.

- ▾ **Bluetooth.** Bluetooth is a wireless technology designed for short distances (up to 33 feet) and slow speeds (1 Mbps). If you have Bluetooth installed on your laptop, *and* if your mobile phone is Bluetooth-enabled, *and* if your mobile phone service plan includes Internet access, you can connect to the Internet with your mobile phone; the phone communicates via Bluetooth with your laptop. This is a nifty way to connect to the Internet when you're on the go, but still within range of your wireless telephone network. See pages 31 and 47–49 for details about how to get connected to your Bluetooth phone.

- ▾ **Network Port Configurations.** This is the pane where you can turn different connection methods on or off, plus arrange the order in which you want your Mac to try to connect. See page 28.

Tip: No matter how you connect, make sure you read page 28 about the Network Port Configurations.

In the Network status pane, you see to the left of each connection a small, colored dot. The color of the dot indicates the connection status via that particular method:

Green dot. The connection is active.

Red dot. The connection is off.

Yellow dot. The device is on, but is not connected to the Internet.

Click the "Show" pop-up menu (shown to the right) to choose any current connection option and show the settings for that connection, as shown on the following pages. Or click one of the connections in the Network Status pane to highlight it, then click the "Configure..." button below to see the settings for that connection.

See the following page to learn about Network Port Configurations.

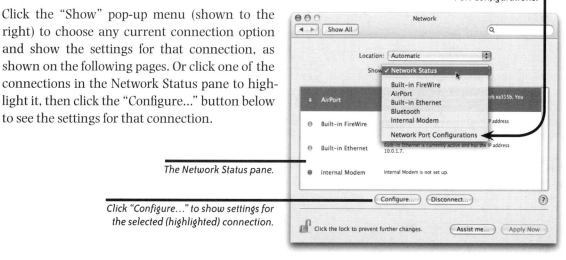

The Network Status pane.

Click "Configure..." to show settings for the selected (highlighted) connection.

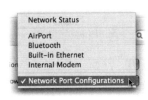

The Network Port Configurations pane

The last item in the "Show" pop-up menu is "Network Port Configurations," but we're talking about it first because it's quite imporant. In this pane *you* determine which network and Internet connection options you want the Mac to use and in which order.

More than one configuration can be turned on at the same time. Why would you need more than one? Well, you might be connected through an Ethernet local area network to other computers in your home and office, plus you might have the only AirPort card in your office, and perhaps you have a phone with an occasional Bluetooth connection.

When your computer attempts to connect to a network or the Internet, it first tries the top item in the list of configurations that you have checked, as shown below. If that connection doesn't succeed, it goes to the next item in the list.

There are two main reasons to be aware of this pane. One, you need to check the options you want to use or they won't show up in the Status pane. Two, if you're having trouble connecting, the first troubleshooting technique is to make sure your desired connection is at the top of the list.

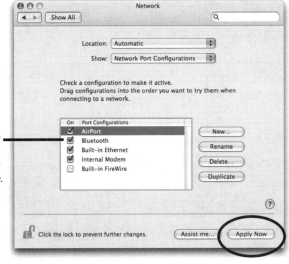

Only the configurations that are checked will appear in the "Show" menu and in the Network Status pane.

To make a configuration active, click the checkbox to put a check in it. Then click the "Apply Now" button.

To rearrange the priority of configurations, drag the items in the list into the order you want your Mac to try to connect (just press on the name and drag it up or down; you'll see a black line that indicates where it will be placed when you let go). For instance, at home you might connect your laptop through an Ethernet broadband connection, but at the coffee shop you connect to the wireless service. At different times, you might want your Mac to first try to connect through one or the other.

Note: The "Built-in FireWire" option enables you to network to another computer via a FireWire cable.

Alternate options for new configurations

There are extra options hidden in the "New..." pop-up menu (shown below). You probably won't ever need to use these, but if you're on a corporate network, your system administrator might advise you to use them.

▼ **6 to 4.** The "6 to 4" option enables connections between computers using IPv4 (which currently includes most everyone) and computers using IPv6 (uncommon now, but coming soon). IPv6 is a new version of Internet Protocol that provides more IP addresses for Internet users than IPv4, the current standard. Although IPv6 is not available to most of us yet, look for it in the near future as IPv4 runs out of available IP numbers for new Internet addresses.

▼ **Link Aggregate.** This option lets you merge two Ethernet ports into one virtual port, providing increased bandwidth.

FYI: IPv4 can support about 4 billion Internet addresses. IPv6 (also known as IPng—Internet Protocol next generation) can support about 3.4 duodecillion Internet addresses.

3.4 duodecillion = 34 trillion trillion trillion.

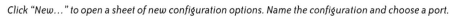
Click "New..." to open a sheet of new configuration options. Name the configuration and choose a port.

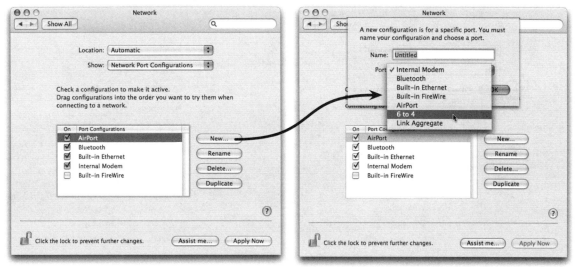

Network configuration for Built-in Ethernet connections

To adjust the settings for a **Built-in Ethernet** configuration, make sure it is checked on in the Network Port Configurations, as explained on page 28. Then either choose "Built-In Ethernet" from the Show menu (shown below), or if you see it in the Status pane, select it and click the "Configure..." button (as shown on page 27).

TCP/IP
Transmission Control Protocol/Internet Protocol:
A set of protocols (procedures) that enable computers to communicate with each other, even if they're not on the same network.

DHCP
Dynamic Host Configuration Protocol:
A protocol that dynamically (on the fly) allocates IP (Internet Protocol) addresses to computers on a network.

▼ **TCP/IP.** The example below shows the TCP/IP pane. **In most situations,** you want to choose "Using DHCP" from the "Configure IPv4" pop-up menu. DHCP automatically allocates an IP address to your computer. *Most users can ignore the rest of this page.*

▼ **PPPoE.** This option (Point-to-Point Protocol over Ethernet) combines dialup connections (PPP) with Ethernet to support multiple users in a local area network. You might find this type of connection in a large office building or apartment complex where many users share a broadband connection and are billed separately. To connect to a network that uses PPPoE, click the tab and enter your account information.

▼ **AppleTalk.** To print to a **PostScript printer,** you need to check the box to "Make AppleTalk Active" in the AppleTalk pane.

▼ **Proxies.** The "Proxies" button lets you configure Proxy Servers if you're on a large network. Check with your network administrator for settings when a firewall or other security measure has been set up.

Choose "Using DHCP" from the "Configure IPv4" pop-up menu. Your Mac automatically configures the Ethernet settings for the Local Area Network (LAN) to which you're currently connected via Ethernet.

If you're having trouble connecting, one trouble-shooting technique is to click this button because your laptop may be trying to use an IP address that is no longer valid. Clicking this button won't hurt anything.

Network configuration for Bluetooth connections

Bluetooth is a short-range (usually about 33 feet maximum) wireless network technology. If your laptop is Bluetooth-enabled, you can use connect it to another Bluetooth device, such as a phone, printer, keyboard, mouse, headset, or handheld PDA. If Bluetooth isn't built in to your computer, you can buy an adapter (shown to the right) and plug it into a USB port.

Set up a Bluetooth mobile phone

For two Bluetooth devices to communicate, you must first *pair* them (see page 47). Keep in mind that to use a Bluetooth-enabled **mobile phone** to connect to the Internet, your mobile phone service plan must include Internet and data access. If you have this plan:

1. First, pair your phone as explained on page 47.

2. Make sure you have Bluetooth checked on, as shown on page 28.

3. In the Network preferences Status pane (shown on page 27), click "Bluetooth," and then click the "Configure..." button.

4. Click the "Bluetooth Modem" tab (circled below).

5. From the "Modem" pop-up menu, choose a modem script that's compatible with your Bluetooth-enabled phone.

For detailed instructions about using your mobile phone to connect your computer to the Internet, see pages 47–51.

FYI: Bluetooth technology is named in honor of King Harald Blåtand (Bluetooth) (940–986 A.D.), a Viking credited with uniting Denmark and Norway and being a positive influence on Scandinavia. Ericsson, a Scandinavian company responsible for developing this short-range, low-power, wireless technology, pays homage to Harald with the name Bluetooth. With standardization, Ericsson aims to unite the field of wireless technology much as Harald Bluetooth united Scandinavia.

King Harald didn't have a blue tooth. The name originated from an old Viking word that meant "dark complexion" (Harald had very dark hair, unusual for a Viking), and the original name has been pronounced "Bluetooth" for hundreds of years.

The Bluetooth company logo (and the icon in your menu bar) is derived from ancient runes for Harald's initials.

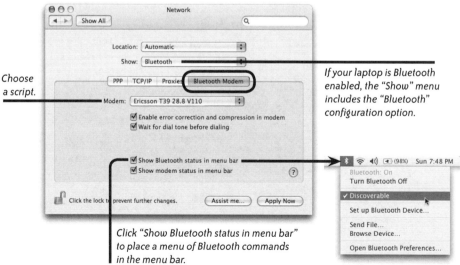

Choose a script.

If your laptop is Bluetooth enabled, the "Show" menu includes the "Bluetooth" configuration option.

Click "Show Bluetooth status in menu bar" to place a menu of Bluetooth commands in the menu bar.

Network configuration for AirPort connections

If your laptop has a wireless card installed *and* there's a wireless base station within range (usually about 150 feet indoors, 300 feet outdoors), your laptop can automatically detect the wireless network and connect to it (unless the network requires a password to join it).

To view settings for the **AirPort** connection (Apple wireless):

1. Make sure you have AirPort checked on, as shown on page 28.

2. From the Show menu (shown below), choose "AirPort."

    Or in the Network preferences Status pane (shown on page 27), click "AirPort," and then click the "Configure..." button.

3. Click the "AirPort" tab (circled below).

The only thing you might need to do here is make sure the box is checked to "Show AirPort status in menu bar." If you check it, then all the options shown on the opposite page are available from the menu bar across the top of your screen.

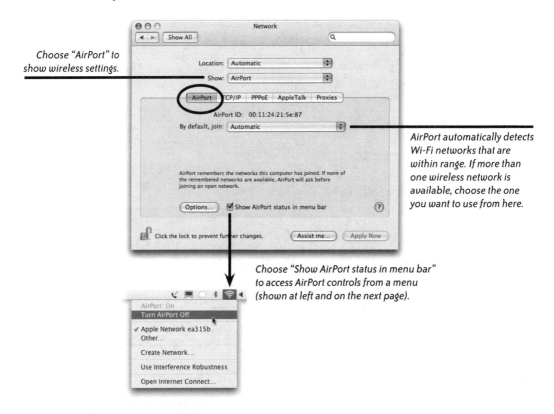

Choose "AirPort" to show wireless settings.

AirPort automatically detects Wi-Fi networks that are within range. If more than one wireless network is available, choose the one you want to use from here.

Choose "Show AirPort status in menu bar" to access AirPort controls from a menu (shown at left and on the next page).

AirPort menu

To access the AirPort connection controls, click the AirPort icon in the menu bar (circled on the right). From this menu, you can:

▼ **Turn AirPort on or off.** To conserve battery power, you can turn AirPort off until you need it. Some places, such as airplanes or hospitals, may prohibit the operation of wireless communication devices; this option allows you to turn off the AirPort but leave your computer on.

▼ **Select a wireless network when more than one is in range.** When your Mac detects multiple wireless networks, all of them automatically appear in this menu. Select the one you want to join.

▼ **Create a temporary local network.** If you and a friend both have Macs with wireless cards, you can connect them to each other wirelessly by creating a computer-to-computer network. Then turn on "Personal File Sharing" (in the Sharing preferences), and Bonjour (part of iChat) will automatically detect the local network and you can share files. **To set up the network,** choose "Create Network"; the window below opens:

Click the AirPort icon in the menu bar to access AirPort controls or to open Internet Connect.

When you join a computer-to-computer network, the AirPort icon in the menu bar changes to include a tiny computer symbol.

Type a name for the computer-to-computer network. The name will appear in the AirPort menu (shown to the left). It will also appear in the "By default, join" menu (shown on the opposite page).

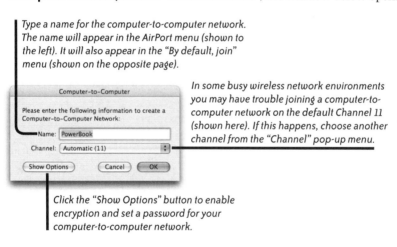

In some busy wireless network environments you may have trouble joining a computer-to-computer network on the default Channel 11 (shown here). If this happens, choose another channel from the "Channel" pop-up menu.

Click the "Show Options" button to enable encryption and set a password for your computer-to-computer network.

Above, you can see the computer-to-computer network I created (named "PowerBook") in my AirPort menu.

▼ **Use Interference Robustness.** If your AirPort signal is weak, selecting this menu item may improve the wireless signal reception. The strength of your wireless reception is indicated by how many arcs of the AirPort icon in the menu bar are black. The AirPort pane of Internet Connect also provides a signal-strength indicator (page 38).

▼ **Open Internet Connect.** Select this option to open Internet Connect, a utility where you can connect to the Internet or modify some of the connection settings. See pages 39–53 for details about Internet Connect.

Network configuration for Internal Modem connections

Another way to connect to the Internet is with your laptop's internal modem. Although dial-up connections are slow, they're usually available when broadband connections are not. But you must have access to a dial-up account, a password, and an ISP (Internet Service Provider) phone number to dial. Connect one end of an ordinary phone cable (RJ-11) to your laptop's modem port and the other end to a phone jack. The **Internal Modem** pane (below) can do the rest.

To change the Internal Modem settings:

1. Make sure you have "Internal Modem" checked on, as shown on page 28.

2. From the Show menu (shown on the opposite page), choose "Internal Modem."

   Or in the Network preferences Status pane (shown on page 27), click "Internal Modem," and then click the "Configure..." button.

3. Click the "PPP" tab (circled, opposite) to display its settings.

4. Enter your ISP dial-up information (account name, password, and the ISP's dial-up number).

5. Click "Apply Now."

6. If you want to dial up right now, click "Dial Now...." Otherwise, you can connect at any time using Internet Connect or a menu option; see page 44.

There are several **disadvantages** of using an internal modem connection. One, of course, is that modem connections are slow compared to broadband connections. However, for Road Warriors, a slow connection is better than no connection.

The other disadvantage is that your computer has to dial the local phone number of your ISP every time you want to connect to the Internet. This is perfectly fine when you're home, but becomes a long-distance expense when away from home. If you think you might need a dial-up connection elsewhere in the world, see page 45 for tips on using a national or international ISP.

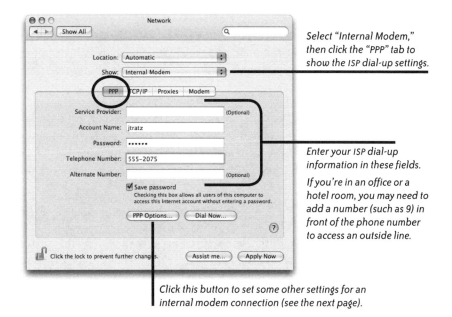

Select "Internal Modem," then click the "PPP" tab to show the ISP dial-up settings.

Enter your ISP dial-up information in these fields.

If you're in an office or a hotel room, you may need to add a number (such as 9) in front of the phone number to access an outside line.

Click this button to set some other settings for an internal modem connection (see the next page).

Dialing modifiers

When the telephone number you enter requires other connections, such as an outside line or credit card calls that have to wait for an automated response, you might need to add a modifier to force the number to pause and wait for a result. Here are some dialing modifiers that can come in handy.

▼ **, (pause for two seconds).** Enter one or more **commas** between numbers to add a pause; each comma equals a two-second pause. If you enter a 9 for an outside line, you might want to put a comma or two after the 9 so it waits long enough (or use the W, as explained below).

▼ **@ (wait for silence).** This modifier after a series of numbers tells the modem to wait for silence on the line (as opposed to a tone) before dialing the remaining numbers.

▼ **& (wait for credit card tone).** When entering a phone card number for dialing, put an ampersand (&) in the series of numbers where you know that the phone card tone signals that it's ready for the next numbers to be entered. The ampersand tells the modem to wait for the credit card tone.

▼ **W (wait for dial tone).** Put this modifier before a series of numbers to make the modem wait for a dial tone before dialing the remaining numbers.

PPP options

When you click the "PPP Options..." button (shown on the previous page), a sheet (shown below) drops down. Most users will be satisfied with the default settings, but here are a couple you might want to think about.

Session Options

▼ **Connect automatically when needed.** This button is particularly useful for dial-up users on Mac OS X because your Mac wants to go to the Internet all the time to access help files, the dictionary, Dashboard items, and much more. It can do so automatically if you check this button.

▼ **Disconnect if idle for [10] minutes.** If your connection quits on you too often (usually because it thinks you've left the room when actually you're sitting right there writing an email), change this to a higher number of minutes. Or *uncheck* the box to disable the function completely. Your ISP can still terminate your connection when it feels you've been on too long.

Advanced Options

We've never had a reason to modify these settings, and they're useful mostly for troubleshooting by network administrators. For instance, if you check "Use verbose logging," your Mac will create large (verbose) log files of your Internet activity, something only a network administrator can appreciate.

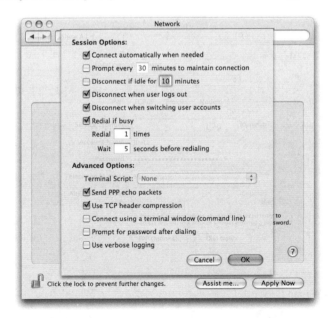

TCP/IP options

Click the "TCP/IP" tab at the top of the Internal Modem pane to check the configuration settings for your modem connection. You probably never need to open this; the only option you might ever use is the "Configure IPv4" menu:

- ▼ **Manually.** If you need to connect using a network modem, choose this option, then enter the IP address for the network modem.
- ▼ **Using PPP.** To connect to an ISP *other than* AOL (America Online), choose this option. It was automatically chosen for you when you when through the original setup process on your Mac.
- ▼ **AOL Dialup.** To connect to an existing AOL account, choose this option.

Be sure to click "Apply Now" if you change any settings.

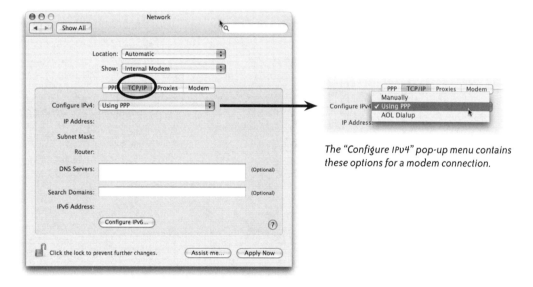

The "Configure IPv4" pop-up menu contains these options for a modem connection.

Proxies

The Proxies tab (shown above, to the right of the circled TCP/IP button) opens a pane in which you can set a proxy server. This is a security feature for connecting through a network that has a firewall set up to protect the privacy of information on the server. If you need to configure a proxy server, get the information you need from the network administrator.

Modem

The "Modem" pane reveals some useful and important settings. The "Modem" pop-up menu contains a list of modem scripts that control how your modem connects to the Internet. It's a very long list of scripts, many of which are designed to work with modem brands other than the Apple Internal modem built in to your Mac laptop.

Don't change this setting unless **you just cannot get connected using the default setting.** Sometimes you can't get connected because the phone lines in your area have been compromised by old age, or because the phone company has for many years (in some cases) *split* phone lines to share them rather than install *new* lines as demand increased. This was okay for a long time because ordinary voice transmission requires much less speed and line quality than is needed for today's high-tech data transmission.

If you're sure your settings are correct, but the connection isn't working, select one of the other modem scripts from the pop-up menu that is *slower*—one that has a similar name to the default script, but has a *lower number*. In the example below, the default modem script has "(v.92)" at the end. The v.92 is a version of the script designed to provide the fastest connection possible on a 56K modem. Choose instead the (v.90) script, as if for a slower connection. If the connection still doesn't work, try the (v.34) script, which is even slower.

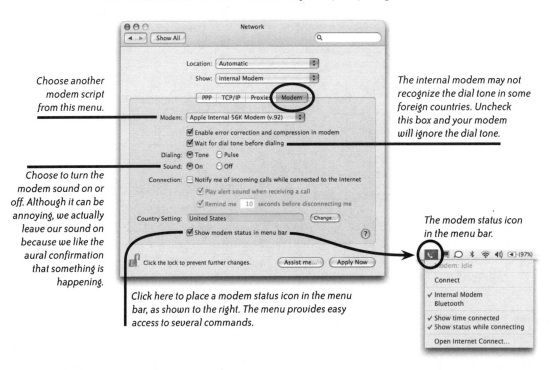

Choose another modem script from this menu.

The internal modem may not recognize the dial tone in some foreign countries. Uncheck this box and your modem will ignore the dial tone.

Choose to turn the modem sound on or off. Although it can be annoying, we actually leave our sound on because we like the aural confirmation that something is happening.

The modem status icon in the menu bar.

Click here to place a modem status icon in the menu bar, as shown to the right. The menu provides easy access to several commands.

Internet Connect

Internet Connect, located in the Applications folder, can help you connect to the Internet in a variety of ways. Use it to connect to a specific wireless network when more than one is available, or to a VPN (Virtual Private Network). Click an icon in the toolbar to see the settings for that particular type of Internet connection. Exactly which Internet connection icons appear in the toolbar is determined by whether or not your Mac detects certain hardware (AirPort, Bluetooth, internal modem) and which options are turned on (active) in the Network preferences (see page 28).

The Internet Connect icon is a network orb with an Ethernet port in the middle.

To open Internet Connect, do one of the following:

▼ In your Applications folder, find and double-click the "Internet Connect" icon.

▼ Or: if you see the modem status icon in the menu bar, from its menu choose "Open Internet Connect..." (circled, below). (If you don't have the modem status icon in your menu bar, see the bottom of the opposite page.)

Modem status icon in the menu bar.

The Internet Connect window

The Internet Connect window (shown below) has various icons in the toolbar; click an icon to display specific information and settings. Exactly which icons appear in the toolbar is determined by the configurations you have checked on in the Network Port Configurations pane, shown on page 28.

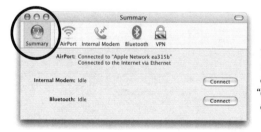

The Summary pane shows the connection status of each configuration and provides "Connect" buttons for idle connections.

—continued

AirPort configurations

To show the status and signal level of an existing Wi-Fi (wireless) connection, single-click the "AirPort" icon in the Internet Connect toolbar. The "Network" menu, shown below, contains the names of all Wi-Fi networks that are in range and have been automatically detected.

To connect to a specific, password-protected wireless network:

1. Open Internet Connect (see the previous page).

2. Choose "Other..." from the "Network" pop-up menu (**A**).

3. From the sheet that drops down (**B**), select a wireless security protocol from the "Wireless Security" pop-up menu (**C**). You must get this information, plus the network name and password, from the wireless network administrator.

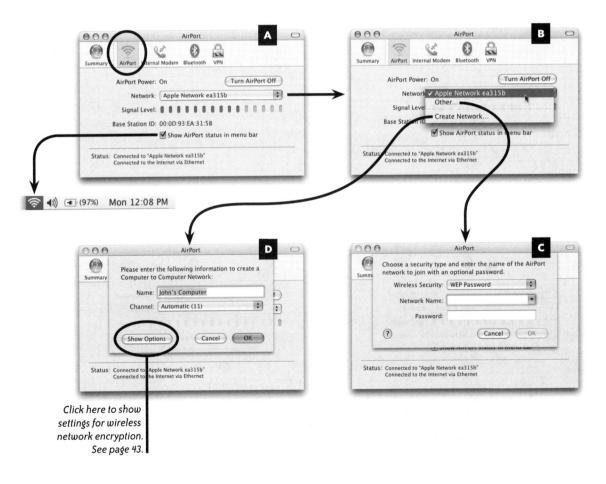

Click here to show settings for wireless network encryption. See page 43.

AirPort icon in menu bar

To place an AirPort icon in the menu bar, as shown to the right, click the "Show AirPort status in menu bar" checkbox (**A** on opposite page).

Click the icon in the menu bar to access a list of commands. Wireless networks within range of your laptop are listed in this menu; a checkmark indicates the network to which you are currently connected.

Computer-to-computer networks

You can create a computer-to-computer network (also known as an *ad hoc network*), in which your computer becomes a wireless base station, also known as an *access point*, A computer-to-computer network is useful for temporary wireless connections to nearby computers when another type of connection is not available.

For instance, perhaps you and your friend are in a coffee shop with wireless access or you've met a business associate in the corporate headquarters where there's a wireless connection and you need to share some files. Create a temporary computer-to-computer wireless network, turn on Personal File Sharing in the Sharing preferences, then use iChat and Bonjour to send files back and forth.

To create a computer-to-computer wireless network:

1. Open the application Internet Connect.
2. Click the "AirPort" icon (**A**, opposite page).
3. From the "Network" pop-up menu (**B**, opposite page), choose "Create Network...."
4. In the sheet that drops down (**D**, opposite page), type a network name or use the default name that appears.

The network name that you created will show up in the "Network" pop-up menu both in Internet Connect and in the AirPort menu across the top of your screen. Other wireless users that are within range can select your network name on their Macs and join your computer-to-computer network.

Changing channels

With a wireless computer-to-computer connection, the default channel "Automatic (11)" should work in most cases. If it doesn't work or if the connection is unusually slow, it's probably due to interference caused by an existing nearby wireless network using the same channel, or one that's too close (such as channel 9 or 10). In this case, select another channel from the pop-up menu that's as far from the existing network's channel as possible. For instance, if the existing wireless network uses channel 10, set your computer-to-computer network to use channel 1.

If you're the administrator of the existing wireless network, you can check to see which channel the base station is using.

1. Open the AirPort Admin Utility, located in the Utilities folder (inside the Applications folder).

2. Select a base station shown in the list.

3. Click the "Configure" icon in the toolbar (shown below) to open the settings pane.

4. In the window that opens, click the "AirPort" button.

5. At the bottom of the window, the "Channel" pop-up menu shows the wireless channel being used by the base station.

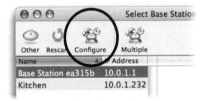

Security

For security reasons, you may want to encrypt your wireless network and require a password to join it.

1. Open Internet Connect (see page 39).

2. From the "Network" pop-up menu (**B** on page 40), choose "Create Network...."

3. Click the "Show Options" button in the bottom-left corner of the "Create Network..." sheet (**D** on page 40). The sheet expands to show encryption settings, as shown below.

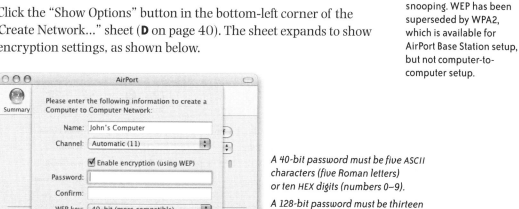

A 40-bit password must be five ASCII characters (five Roman letters) or ten HEX digits (numbers 0–9).

A 128-bit password must be thirteen ASCII characters or 26 HEX digits.

WEP (Wired Equivalent Privacy) is a part of the wireless 802.11 standard that provides security for wireless networks. WEP is, however, a minimal level of security to deter snooping. WEP has been superseded by WPA2, which is available for AirPort Base Station setup, but not computer-to-computer setup.

4. Click the "Enable encryption" checkbox.

5. Type a password, then confirm it by typing it again in the next field.

6. Choose a "WEP key" (40-bit or 128-bit). The 40-bit is more compatible with other computers, and the 128-bit is more secure.

Internal Modem configurations

The Internal Modem pane (shown below) is where you set the telephone number, your account name, and the password for the dial-up account you want to use. You can create several configurations so you can easily connect to different ISPs while traveling (see page 47 about dial-up numbers).

To modify settings for a dial-up connection to the Internet:

1. Make sure "Internal Modem" has been checked on in the Network Port Configurations pane (see page 28).

2. Open Internet Connect (see page 39).

3. Click the "Internal Modem" icon in the Internet Connect toolbar, as shown below.

4. Enter the ISP telephone number, your account name, and the password for the account. Keep in mind that these are not necessarily the same as your email account name and password! Ask your ISP for the exact information to enter if you're not sure.

5. If you want to connect right now, click the "Connect" button.

Check this box to place a modem icon in the main menu bar, as shown below.

Modem status icon in menu bar

To place a modem status icon in the menu bar, as shown below, click the box to "Show modem status in menu bar" (shown above).

Click the icon in the menu bar to access a list of commands, as shown below. This makes it easy to connect and to open Internet Connect with a click.

Dial-up number while traveling

When you're traveling, a phone line may be the only type of connection available. You *could* add 1 plus the area code to the telephone number to connect (long distance) to your local ISP back home. But long distance is expensive, and the phone (belonging to your friend, associate, or hotel) will be charged the long-distance fees.

Instead, create a **new configuration**, as described on the following page, using *local* ISP information (perhaps your friend has an ISP). You can set up additional configurations for any other modem locations that you use regularly.

▾ **Local ISP.** Many local ISPs provide a list of nationwide local telephone access numbers that you can use while on the go. Check your ISP's web site to see if they offer this service. Some local ISPs may also have special instructions for accessing their service from remote locations, such as adding the ISP's domain name to your ISP login name. For example, a login name of *tiger* may change to *tiger@ISPname.com.* Your service provider should have this information on their web site. If not, call them and ask.

At **TheList.com** (an ISP buyer's guide), you can search for an ISP by location, area code, Canada nationwide, or U.S. nationwide.

▾ **National ISP.** Most national ISPs provide local phone access numbers for most major urban areas in the U.S. If you're considering a national ISP, such as EarthLink or NetZero, check their web site to make sure they provide telephone access numbers for the areas in which you intend to travel. EarthLink offers an 800 service so you can connect using a toll-free number in U.S. areas that are too remote to have an EarthLink local access number. The 800 service is pay-as-you-go, and your account will be billed an *additional* 10 cents per minute ($6 an hour) for usage. If you plan to use the EarthLink 800 service, contact them in advance to receive your number.

A few national ISPs:
EarthLink.net
FasterMacs.net
NetZero.net

▾ **International ISP.** An ISP such as EarthLink can also provide international roaming services that allow you to connect to the Internet with dial-up when you're outside of your home country. EarthLink's web site provides a list of international access phone numbers that you can use if you have an EarthLink account. EarthLink International Roaming costs 15 cents per minute ($9 an hour) *in addition* to your monthly fee.

A few international ISPs:
EarthLink.net
Dialer.net

TheList.com provides information about ISPs around the world.

Search the web for "global roaming service" or "international ISP."

Also see page 35 for important information about dialing modifiers that come in handy if you need to use a calling card number or if you need to get an outside line. And see Chapter 8 for more tips on roaming around the world.

Multiple configurations for dialing ISPs

As we mentioned on the previous page, you can create different configurations for different ISP accounts so you can quickly and easily connect using another ISP. For instance, you might have a dial-up number to use at your sister's house in Alamo, one to get through the motel switchboard in Starkville, and another to use in your London apartment.

To create a new modem configuration:

1. In the Internal Modem pane, click on the "Configuration" pop-up menu, then choose "Edit Configurations...."

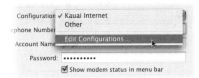

2. Click the Add button (the plus sign) to make a new configuration. You'll notice that the current configuration's settings are still displayed in the text fields, as shown below.

3. In the "Description" field, type a name for the new configuration. Add the new ISP telephone number, account name, and password to the other text fields.

If the modem script you select supports manual dialing, you can enable it here. Then when you connect, a message window appears on the screen and instructs you to pick up the phone and manually dial the phone number.

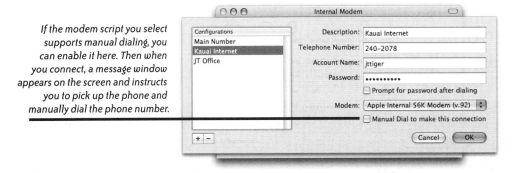

4. Click OK and your new config will be added to the list on the left of this sheet, and to the modem status menu bar across the top of your screen so you can connect to it with a single click.

Bluetooth configurations

Bluetooth is a wireless technology designed for short distances (up to 33 feet), and is ideal for connecting to a nearby Bluetooth-enabled mobile phone, PDA, or other Bluetooth device, such as a hands-free headset. Your laptop might have Bluetooth built-in; if not, you can buy a Bluetooth module that plugs into the USB port on your computer (see a photo on page 31).

Pair your device

Once Bluetooth is on your computer, its icon should automatically appear in your menu bar, as shown here (if not, see below). A Bluetooth device must be *paired* with your laptop before you can use it. **To pair it,** go to the Bluetooth menu, choose "Set up Bluetooth Device...," and follow the simple directions.

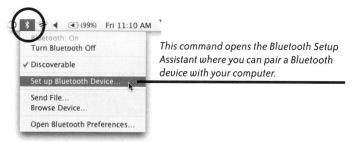

This command opens the Bluetooth Setup Assistant where you can pair a Bluetooth device with your computer.

To place the Bluetooth icon in the menu bar (if it isn't there already):

1. Make sure "Bluetooth" has been checked on in the Network Port Configurations pane (see page 28).
2. Open Internet Connect (see page 39).
3. Click the "Bluetooth" icon in the toolbar, as shown below.
4. Put a checkmark in "Show modem status in menu bar."

Bluetooth preferences

Don't forget to peruse the Bluetooth preferences (open System Preferences and click on the Bluetooth icon). If you use a Bluetooth mouse or keyboard with your laptop, you probably want to check the option to allow devices to wake your computer. And if you find that the connection to your keyboard or mouse gets broken every time your start your Mac, check the box to open the Bluetooth Setup Assistant on startup so it will connect them automatically.

Set up a Bluetooth configuration

After pairing a Bluetooth-enabled mobile phone with your laptop, as described on the previous page, you can set up a configuration in Internet Connect that allows your mobile phone to act as a modem and connect your laptop to the Internet—*if* your particular mobile phone plan provides Internet connectivity and data communication. If not, you can usually add that service for an additional monthly fee.

To set up a Bluetooth modem configuration for your phone:

1. Make sure "Bluetooth" has been checked on in the Network Port Configurations pane (see page 28).

2. Make sure you have paired your phone (see page 48).

3. Open Internet Connect (see page 39).

4. Click the "Bluetooth" icon in the Internet Connect toolbar, as shown below.

The phone number was added automatically when I paired my Sony-Ericsson mobile phone to my laptop. However, my phone model didn't work with any of the included modem scripts.

The following pages describe how I made a successful connection by downloading and installing additional modem scripts that I found on the web.

If the Bluetooth icon isn't showing in this toolbar, it probably isn't checked on in the Network Port Configurations.

5. The process of pairing your Bluetooth phone might have automatically filled in the text fields shown above. If not, fill in the phone number, account name, and password.

6. To test the configuration, make sure your phone is on, then click the "Connect" button.

7. If your connection is successful, the Internet Connect pane will expand to show you the connection status, as shown below.

This expanded pane shows your connection status. Click the "Disconnect" button to terminate the connection.

Tip: Browsing the Internet on your laptop through a mobile phone connection can be expensive because many mobile phone plans charge *per bit* of downloaded data, which includes text and graphics on a web page. You can save money (and speed up page downloads) if you *turn off graphics* in your web browser before making a connection. (In Safari, turn off graphics in the Appearance preferences.)

Road Warrior modem scripts

Unfortunately, there's a very good chance that your connection attempt will *not* be successful due to incompatibility between your particular mobile phone and the modem scripts that happen to be in the Modem Scripts folder (located in the Library folder). A casual user might give up in a situation like this, concluding that Bluetooth Internet connections are not really necessary. But we're Road Warriors, right? We know there will be a day when we desperately want to check our email from a rest stop just outside of NoPlaceSpecial, far away from telephone lines and Wi-Fi hotspots. Or, more likely, we'll just want to impress someone else in the car. If our mobile phone can reach our wireless mobile phone network, we can connect. So let's do some Road Warrior stuff.

To download, install, and use additional modem scripts:

1. From the Internet, download a collection of freeware modem scripts. We recommend those available at *Ross Barkman's Home Page* (www. taniwha.org.uk). The web page provides links to scripts for many different mobile phone brands.

Since we own a Sony Ericsson T610 phone, we downloaded the "Sony Ericsson GPRS Scripts." The download included a collection of ten scripts and a ReadMe file containing instructions and some valuable tips for Network and PPP settings, as shown on the following page.

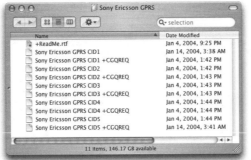

While this example is specific to Sony Ericsson mobile phones, it does provide an overview of the connection process for any Bluetooth-enabled mobile phone.

This is the folder of Sony Ericsson scripts we downloaded.

Be sure to read the included ReadMe file for some very important step-by-step instructions and tips.

2. Find your "Modem Scripts" folder—it's in the *computer's* Library folder (not your *user* Library folder that you see in your Home window). Drag the scripts into the computer's "Modem Scripts" folder.

Of course, we assume you have gone into the Network Port Configurations in the Network preferences and checked the box to turn on Bluetooth. See page 28.

3. Check the Network preferences to make sure the new scripts are available:

    a. Open System Preferences and click the "Network" icon.

    b. From the "Show" menu at the top of the dialog box, choose "Bluetooth."

    c. In the pane that appears, click the "Bluetooth" tab

    d. Click the "Modem" menu in the middle of the dialog box and see if your new scripts are in the list.

If you don't see the new scripts, restart your Mac.

4. Open Internet Connect (it's in your Applications folder).

5. Click the Bluetooth icon in the toolbar to show its pane (shown below).

As shown above, the text fields in the Configuration pane may already contain information that was put there automatically when you paired your Bluetooth-enabled phone. Ignore these settings and create a *new* configuration, as explained on the opposite page.

6. From the "Configuration" menu, choose "Edit Configurations…" to reveal the Configurations sheet, as shown below.

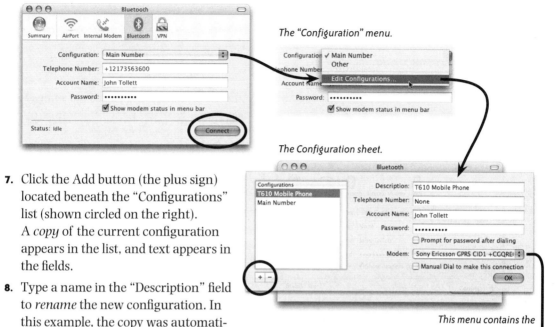

The "Configuration" menu.

The Configuration sheet.

This menu contains the new scripts that you placed in the Modem Scripts folder, in addition to all of the original modem scripts.

7. Click the Add button (the plus sign) located beneath the "Configurations" list (shown circled on the right). A *copy* of the current configuration appears in the list, and text appears in the fields.

8. Type a name in the "Description" field to *rename* the new configuration. In this example, the copy was automatically named "Main Number Copy"; I renamed it "T610 Mobile Phone."

9. In the "Telephone Number" field, type "None." The phone number is already included in the new modem script that you downloaded.

10. Enter your phone's mobile service account name and password.

11. From the "Modem" menu, choose one of the new modem scripts you downloaded. You don't know which one works yet, so choose the first one in the list.

12. Click OK to close the sheet.

13. In the Internet Connect window (shown at the top), click "Connect."

If the connection is successful, the window expands to show the connection status, as shown on page 49.

If the connection fails, go back to Step 4. From the "Configuration" menu, select the configuration you just added to the list. Choose a *different* script from the "Modem" menu (above-right). Click OK, then click "Connect" to try this new one.

If the connection fails again, try *another* new script from the "Modem" menu until you find the one that works.

VPN configurations

A VPN (Virtual Private Network) is a private communications network that uses a public network (the Internet). Many large companies use VPN technology so that employees can use the Internet to securely access their company's private internal network. It can be very handy to be able to connect to your company's network while lounging in Fiji—I mean, while taking notes at a business meeting.

If you're not part of a large organization that uses VPN, you won't need any of these settings. If you do have access to a VPN, the network administrator will give you the information you need for the panes shown here.

To set up a VPN configuration

L2TP (Layer 2 Tunneling Protocol) and **PPTP** (Point-to-Point Tunneling Protocol) are protocols that network administrators use to securely join different networks, using the Internet as an intermediary.

IPSec (Internet Protocol Security) adds strong security to L2TP and is called **L2TP over IPSec**.

1. Open Internet Connect (it's in your Applications folder).

2. Click the "VPN" icon in the Internet Connect toolbar. You are immediately asked to select the kind of VPN you want: *L2TP over IPSec* or *PPTP*.

Choose a VPN network type, then click "Continue" to close this sheet.

3. Your network administrator will supply the correct information to place in the blank fields. She may even set it up for you.

An L2TP network.

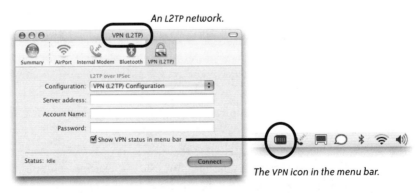

The VPN icon in the menu bar.

To edit an existing VPN config or to add a new one, from the "Configuration" menu choose "Edit Configurations...." The edit sheet (shown below) drops down. Ask your network administator to provide the information you need. After your settings are made, click OK.

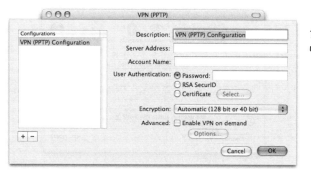

This VPN Configuration sheet opens when you select "Edit Configurations...."

Turn off the VPN configuration

When you set up a VPN configuration, it is added to the list of network connections. You can see these in the Network Port Configurations pane of the Network preferences (see pages 26–28), as shown below. **To turn off the VPN configuration,** uncheck its box, then click "Apply Now."

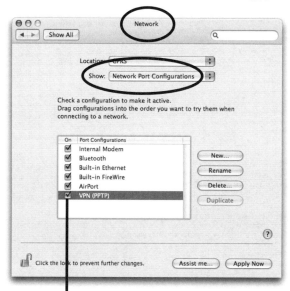

To turn a configuration on or off, check or uncheck its box.

To force your Mac to try to connect through the VPN before it tries any other config, drag the VPN name to the top of the list.

Set up Customized Network Locations

A network *location* is nothing more than a preset group of network settings that are customized for certain locations where you regularly need to connect to the Internet.

Create an online location

For instance, you can create a new location named "Home," then choose the network settings needed to connect from that location. You can create another location named "School" or "Office" and choose settings that are customized for the way you connect at those locations (dial-up, Ethernet, Wi-Fi, etc.). Then with the click of a menu item, you can switch the location settings from one connection to another.

To create a new location:

1. From the Apple menu, choose System Preferences, or click the System Preferences icon in the Dock. Then click the "Network" icon.

2. From the "Location" pop-up menu, choose "New Location...."

3. Enter a name for the new location, as shown below. Click OK.

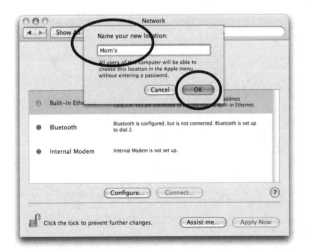

4. From the "Show" pop-up menu, choose the type of connection to use at the new location (internal modem, Ethernet, AirPort, etc.).

5. Enter settings for the various text fields and menus that apply to your chosen connection type.

6. Click "Apply Now."

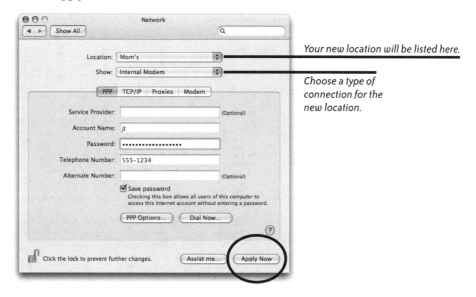

Your new location will be listed here.

Choose a type of connection for the new location.

Create an offline location

Sometimes when you're on the go, automatic Internet connection attempts by certain software applications can be annoying or inconvenient. If you don't want your computer to connect to the Internet when you open Mail or your web browser (or other programs that attempt to connect automatically), create a new location that turns off the connectivity.

To create an offline location:

1. Create a new location as explained above. Name the location something like "Offline."

2. From the "Show" menu, select "Network Port Configurations."

3. Uncheck every checkbox to turn off all of the network ports (Built-in Ethernet, Internal Modem, AirPort, etc.), as shown on the following page.

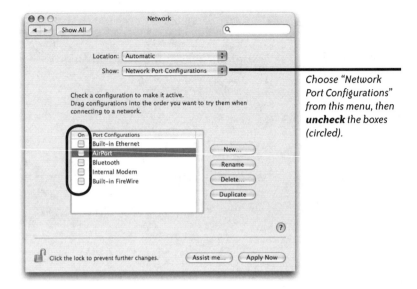

Choose "Network Port Configurations" from this menu, then **uncheck** the boxes (circled).

4. Click "Apply Now."

Your computer won't be able to connect to the Internet when you choose this location from the "Location" menu.

Select your location from the Apple menu

1. From the Apple menu, choose "Location."

2. From the "Location" sub-menu (shown below), choose the location you want to use.

3. Now your Network preferences are automatically set to that location's customized settings.

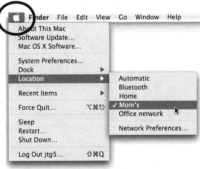

A .Mac Account
for Mobile Computing

Some Mac users still don't realize how useful it is to have a .Mac (pronounced "dot Mac") account. We'll make sure you're not one of them. At $99.95/year, it's an incredible value, especially for people on the go. This chapter explores the ways that a .Mac account can help keep you connected to family, friends, and other important associates. A .Mac membership also gives you access to members-only technical support, free software, special deals on selected software, and exclusive tutorials.

- ▼ **iDisk.** Your iDisk is personal data storage on Apple servers. Use it to store files you will need while traveling or between home and office. See pages 59–64.

- ▼ **iSync.** Synchronize Address Book information, iCal calendars, Safari bookmarks, passwords, and Mail accounts between multiple Macs so your traveling laptop has the same contact information as your desktop Mac. See pages 65–70.

- ▼ **.Mac Mail.** Get and send email from any computer and any browser. See pages 71–74.

- ▼ **.Mac Address Book.** Access your Address Book on any computer in the world. See pages 75–77.

- ▼ **.Mac Bookmarks.** Access your personal Safari bookmarks from any computer and almost any browser. See pages 78–81.

- ▼ **.Mac Groups.** Share messages, files, photos, movies, and a calendar on a private Group web page. See pages 82–85.

- ▼ **.Mac Slides.** Create and publish slideshows while you're on the go. Other Mac OS X users can subscribe to your slideshow and it appears as screen savers on their Macs. when you change your slideshow, their screen savers change. See pages 86–87.

- ▼ **iWeb.** Create and publish web pages with a blog, photos, and movies. See pages 88–95.

- ▼ **Photocasting.** Publish an album of your images from iPhoto so others can subscribe to them. As you update your album, the subscribers' iPhoto albums also update. See pages 96–97.

- ▼ **Backup.** Use the Backup application to archive files to a location on your computer, to removable discs, external drives, or to your iDisk. See pages 98–100.

A .Mac Account

 .mac

.Mac is a collection of tools and services that are available when you subscribe to a .Mac membership from Apple. It costs $99.95 per year.

If you don't have a .Mac account, you're missing out on some great Road Warrior advantages!

A **.Mac membership** includes one gigabyte of combined email and iDisk space (storage on Apple's servers), and you can choose to buy up to one additional gigabyte. You can determine how much of your iDisk space is allocated for email and how much for other storage.

The **.Mac Family Pack** ($179.95 a year) includes one full .Mac membership with one gigabyte of storage, as well as four sub-accounts with 250 megabytes of storage, and a shared iDisk folder for you and your family.

Try the free trial—and keep the email address

A sixty-day free .Mac trial is available, complete with an email address that you can keep even after your free trial is up. You also get fifty megabytes of storage space. The free trial includes limited versions of some .Mac features.

Sign up!

To sign up, go to **www.Mac.com** and click "Join Now."

iDisk

As a .Mac member, you have instant access to your **iDisk**—one gigabyte of personal storage (including email storage) on Apple's servers. You can upgrade your iDisk storage capacity at any time (for a fee), up to four gigabytes.

Your .Mac uses iDisk to make its best features a reality: web site publishing, photocasting, backup protection, synchronization of calendars and address books, slideshow screen savers, and whatever else Apple's innovative imagination may offer in the future.

How does your Mac know which iDisk to open?

How does your Mac know which iDisk is yours? After you set up an account, your member name and password appear in the .Mac preferences as shown below (click the "System Preferences" icon in your Dock, then click the ".Mac" icon). You can see below the .Mac member name and password. iDisk opens the account currently shown in this pane.

Set (or change) your .Mac account information in this window.

Put iDisk on your Desktop

You can "mount" your iDisk so it appears on your Desktop just like any hard disk, then copy files between your Mac and the iDisk—you are really copying files from your Mac to Apple's server (or vice versa). Once files are on your iDisk (on the Apple computer), you can access them anywhere in the world. Directions on how to open your iDisk and use it are on the following page.

To open your iDisk, do one of the following:

▼ **Finder window.** Click the iDisk icon in a Finder window Sidebar (shown to the left).

If the iDisk icon does not appear in the Sidebar: From the Finder menu, choose "Preferences...." Click the "Sidebar" icon in the toolbar. Make sure that "iDisk" has a check next to it.

▼ **Go menu.** From the Go menu in the Finder, choose "iDisk," then choose "My iDisk" from the submenu.

If you don't see the Go menu in the menu bar, you are not at the Finder—just click on any blank space you see of the Desktop and that will take you to the Finder.

Tip: If you're not using a broadband connection, connecting to your iDisk can take time. Make sure you are connected to the Internet before you go to your iDisk.

You can access a different iDisk without changing your .Mac preferences:

1. From the Go menu in the Finder, choose "iDisk."
2. From the submenu, choose "Other User's iDisk...."
3. Enter the name and password of your other account, or of someone else's account if they've given you the password.

When you open your iDisk, its icon appears on your Desktop and a window opens that shows your iDisk content (both shown below). Amazing.

dearrobin

This icon appears on your Desktop, named with your .Mac member name.

This window is your iDisk. Anything you put in these folders is stored on Apple's computers.

As you do .Mac things like publish a HomePage, create a site in iWeb, put up a Photocast, create a Group, etc., Apple stores the files for it on your iDisk.

To open someone's Public folder:

marysidney-Public

1. From the Go menu in the Finder, choose "iDisk."
2. From the submenu, choose "Other User's Public Folder...."
3. Enter the name of a .Mac member. An icon, as shown to the left, appears on your Desktop; double-click it. If there are files in that person's Public folder, you can see them in the window.

iDisk Contents

When you double-click the **iDisk** icon on your Desktop to open its window, as shown on the previous page, you're actually looking at files and folders that are on Apple's server. This explains why the window is sometimes slow to open (especially if you're using a dial-up connection instead of broadband).

All of your iDisk folders are **private** and accessible only to you (or someone who knows your password), except the folder called "Public."

- ▾ **Backup folder.** When you use Backup, Apple's software for .Mac members (see pages 98–100), this folder on your iDisk is where the archived files are stored.

- ▾ **Documents folder.** Drag into this folder any kind of document that you want to store and make available to yourself over the Internet.

- ▾ **Library folder.** The Library folder contains application support files. Anything that needs to be in this folder will automatically be placed there. Don't drag files into or out of this folder.

- ▾ **Movies folder.** Drag movies that you might use in a HomePage web site into this iDisk Movies folder so you'll have access to them when you're building the web page—or for anything else.

- ▾ **Music folder.** Drag music files and playlists to this private iDisk folder so you can have access to them from anywhere in the world.

- ▾ **Pictures folder.** Drag individual photos or a folder of photos that you plan to use in a HomePage web site into this iDisk Pictures folder so you'll have access to them when you're building the web page or for any other reason.

- ▾ **Sites folder.** The Sites folder stores any web pages you've created using HomePage. You can also store sites here that were created with any other web authoring software. For instance, using Dreamweaver, Robin made a simple site she named LibraryAngels and put it in her iDisk Sites folder. You can view the site at homepage.mac.com/ dearrobin/LibraryAngels.

- ▾ **Software folder.** The Software folder contains free software provided to you by Apple, including AppleWorks. If you see anything you want in these folders, drag it to your Desktop. The contents of this folder do not count against your iDisk storage space.

- ▾ **Groups folder.** If you create or join a .Mac Group (pages 82–85), then your Groups folder contains a subfolder with the same name as your Group. Inside that folder are other folders (Documents, Pictures, Movies, etc) into which you drag files to share with other members of the Group. Any files people put in their own Groups folder will appear in yours. Amazing.

▼ **Web folder.** If you use iWeb to create a web site, your files will be stored in here. (However, if you create a web site from a Groups page, as shown on page 84, that web site is stored inside the Groups folder.)

▼ **Public folder.** Put files and folders here that you want to make accessible for other people. Unless you set up password protection (see the opposite page), other people who have your .Mac member name can access files that you drag to your iDisk Public folder. You can open any one else's Public folder that doesn't use password protection if you have that person's .Mac member name.

Save files directly into your iDisk

You don't have to open your iDisk to save files into it. While working in any application, you can go to the Save As dialog box and choose to save the file directly into any folder on your iDisk. We suggest you wait until you're finished with the document before you save it to the iDisk; otherwise, every time you save the slightest change, your Mac will have to access your iDisk on the Apple server to save the change. And you won't have a copy on your own computer.

To save a file directly to your iDisk:

1. Make sure your iDisk icon is showing in your window Sidebar, as explained at the top of page 60.

2. When you're finished working on the document (of course you've been saving it to your computer along the way), go to the File menu and choose "Save As...."

3. In the Sidebar of the Save As window, click the iDisk icon. It might take a minute or two, depending on the speed of your connection. Choose the folder in which you want to save your file, then click "Save."

This is an easy way to save files into your Groups folder on your iDisk, as discussed on page 85.

Manage your iDisk

To manage your iDisk, use the iDisk pane in the .Mac preferences, as shown below. You can monitor your storage allotment, buy more space, set access privileges and password protection for your Public folder, and even copy the contents of your entire iDisk to your laptop in case you want access while offline (you can sync it again when you get connected to a fast connection).

Allowing others to upload files to your Public folder can make it easy for you to get files from associates while you're on the road.

Tip: If you need to access an iDisk from a machine running **Windows XP,** download the free **iDisk Utility for Windows XP.** Installation instructions are included with the download.

You'll find it in the iDisk section of Mac.com.

To monitor your iDisk Storage:

Check here at any time to see how much .Mac storage space you're using and how much you have available. Click "Buy More" to see available options and prices and to purchase more space.

To copy (sync) your entire iDisk to your laptop:

If you know you won't have broadband access for a while on the road, you can copy the contents of your entire iDisk to your laptop; click the "Start" button. That way you have access to all the files. When you have a broadband connection again, you can synchronize the files with Apple's server.

To set access privileges or password protection:

The default is to allow visitors to "read" the files you've put in your Public folder, meaning they cannot change anything in your folder. **To allow others to upload files to the Public folder** on your iDisk, click the "Read & Write" button. You should then add a password—check the box to "Password protect your Public Folder." Type a password in the fields that appear, then click OK.

iDisk Storage Settings

A default .Mac account includes combined email and iDisk storage of 1024 megabytes (which is one gigabyte) on Apple's servers. The total amount of storage is automatically divided evenly between email and iDisk when you start your account, but you can change that ratio if you need more email storage or more iDisk storage.

To re-allocate your iDisk storage settings:

1. Open System Preferences and click the .Mac icon.

2. Click the "Account" tab, if it isn't already.

3. Click the "Account Info" button in the bottom-right corner to open a .Mac web page that contains your "Account Settings."

4. Click the "Storage Settings" button (circled, below-left) to show the management tools.

5. On the "Storage Settings" page, you can see the distribution of your storage space divided between your iDisk and .Mac Mail. If you want to change the settings, choose a different amount from the pop-up menu, as shown below. The allocated amounts will change instantly.

6. When you're done, click "Save."

iSync

With iSync, you can store your contacts, calendars, bookmarks, and other data on the .Mac synchronization server. You can also store your Keychain passwords, Mail accounts, rules, signatures, and Smart Mailboxes. Then with the click of a button you can **synchronize** this information to another Mac.

This process not only allows you to synchronize several Macs, but it also allows you to access certain data on other computers you might use along your travels. For instance, while using Internet Explorer on a PC in an Internet cafe in Bangkok, you can access your Safari bookmarks.

Also, you might add Address Book contacts and iCal information while traveling around with your laptop. You can synchronize that data with your desktop Mac or with family or co-workers back home, even while on the road.

Register your Mac with the .Mac server

The first step, while you're still at home, is to register your main Mac (either your primary desktop Mac or your laptop) with the .Mac server.

To register your Mac to the .Mac server ...

1. Open the System Preferences: Either click its icon in the Dock, or go to the Apple menu and choose "System Preferences...."

2. Click the ".Mac" icon in System Preferences (circled, below-left) to open the .Mac preferences (shown below-right).

You can click the "Advanced" tab to see that your Mac has been registered. You can also unregister it there.

3. Click the "Account" tab (circled above), if it isn't already selected.

4. If your .Mac member name and password are not in the fields, enter them; hit Enter or Return.

—continued

Sync your data

Once you sign in on the .Mac preferences, your Mac is registered to the .Mac synchronization server. Information that you choose to sync (see below) gets copied to that server.

To sync your data to the .Mac server:
(Skip Steps 1 and 2 below if you're still viewing the .Mac preferences from the previous page.)

1. Open the System Preferences: Either click its icon in the Dock, or go to the Apple menu and choose "System Preferences...."

2. Click the ".Mac" icon in System Preferences to open the .Mac preferences.

3. Click the "Sync" tab (circled below) to show the Sync pane.

4. Check the box to "Synchronize with .Mac." then from the menu choose how often you want your computer to sync the selected information.

   Automatically: iSync will sync whenever a change is made to the selected file type.

   Manually: iSync will wait until you click the "Sync Now" button.

5. In the list of icons, check the data you want to sync.

6. Click "Sync Now."

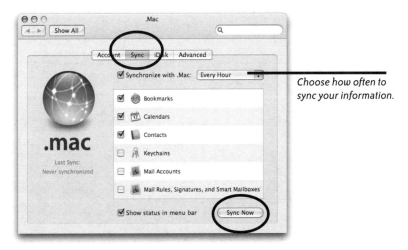

Choose how often to sync your information.

7. When iSync starts, an "Alert" message appears for each of the selected data categories, as shown below.

   From its menu, choose how you want iSync to handle the data, as described below:

 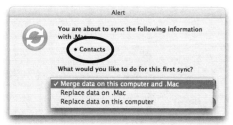

Replace data on this computer: If there's existing data on the .Mac server, it will *replace* the data *on your Mac.*

Replace data on .Mac. This is the option you want to choose when you sync for the first time. It copies the data on your Mac *to the .Mac server.*

Merge data on this computer and .Mac: If there's existing data on the .Mac server, merge it with the data on your Mac. If the Mac finds conflicting data (like two different addresses for the same name), it will ask you what to do.

8. After answering each alert message, click the "Sync" button.

Sync one Mac to another

Many of us work on two or more Macs—perhaps one at the office and one at home, or maybe multiple computers in one office or home. To synchronize all the computers so you have the same information everywhere you go, perform a **Mac-to-Mac synchronization.** In this procedure, the data on the .Mac server is synchronized to a *different* Mac. For instance, perhaps you synced your desktop computer to the .Mac server; you can then transfer all that data onto your laptop.

In the following steps, you are first going to register a *second* computer to the same .Mac account. All computers registered to a specific .Mac account are listed in the "Advanced" pane of .Mac Preferences, as shown here.

iSync picks up the computer name that you entered in the Sharing preferences.

As you can see here, Robin chooses to sync some of her Macs, but not others, depending on where she uses them.

To sync the data to another Mac

1. Make sure you've already synced your main Mac to the .Mac server, as described on the previous pages.

2. On a different Mac, open the .Mac preferences (in the System Preferences).

3. In the "Account" pane, sign in with the same member name and password of the .Mac account whose info you want to sync with.

4. Click the "Sync" tab (shown on page 66). Put a checkmark next to data you want to sync.

5. Click "Sync Now." You may need to resolve conflicts.

Resolve conflicts

If iSync finds a conflict between a file on the .Mac server and a matching but slightly different file on your Mac, "Conflict Resolver" (shown below) opens.

- ▼ **Review Later.** If you choose to "Review Later," then a new item appears in your iSync's status menu (see the following page) called "Review Conflicts Now...." When you're ready, choose that item from the status menu in the menu bar across the top of your screen.

- ▼ **Review Now.** Click this to see the conflicting files, as shown below. Click on the pane that contains the information you want to use in the sync, then click "Done." In the sheet that drops down, choose "Sync Later" or "Sync Now."

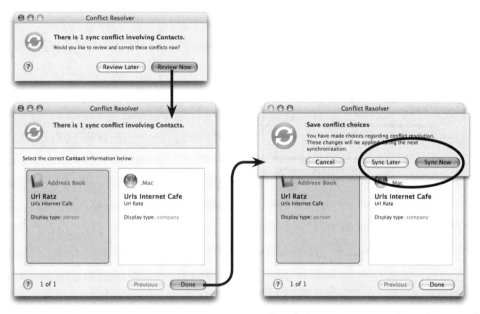

If you don't want to sync now, choose "Sync Later."
Then at some other time you can choose
"Sync Now" from the iSync status menu (next page).

Show iSync status in the menu bar

You can make iSync even more accessible if you put its icon in the menu bar where you can click the icon to open an iSync pop-up menu.

To place the iSync icon in the menu bar:

▼ In the iSync pane of .Mac Preferences (circled below-left), check the box to "Show status in menu bar."

▼ **Or** while the iSync application is open, go to its application menu (just to the right of the blue Apple) and choose "Preferences...." Check the box to "Show status in menu bar" (circled below-right).

When syncing is in progress, this bar animates and the "Sync Now" button turns into "Cancel Sync."

To use the iSync status menu:

▼ From the iSync menu in the menu bar (shown below), choose "Sync Now." **Or** you can directly open the Sync preferences.

If you choose "Sync Now," your files are synchronized using the current settings in the .Mac preferences, but it doesn't open the iSync window. If you want to check the settings or change them, choose "Open .Mac Sync Preferences..." from the menu before you sync.

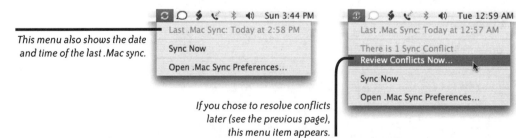

This menu also shows the date and time of the last .Mac sync.

If you chose to resolve conflicts later (see the previous page), this menu item appears.

.Mac Mail

Your .Mac account includes **.Mac Mail** (web-based email). Web-based email enables you to get or send email from any computer that has an Internet connection and a browser. In addition to accessing your .Mac email, you can set it up to check other email accounts you might have.

*Don't get **.Mac Mail** (web-based mail on the Mac.com site) confused with **Mail** (the email application on your computer).*

Email-only .Mac accounts

You can buy additional *email-only* accounts that include fifty megabytes of email storage space for each account. These can come in handy when you're traveling—you can keep all your travel email separate from your personal or business mail to make sure you spend time receiving mail *only* from people who have this special address.

Email-only accounts don't include many of the standard .Mac features such as iDisk, HomePage, Backup, and Bookmarks. But that's probably why they call it email-*only.*

To add an email-only account to your .Mac membership, go to Mac.com and click the "Account" link in the web page's sidebar. In the Account page that opens, click the "Buy More" button.

POP vs. IMAP accounts

.Mac Mail uses an Internet standard called **IMAP** (Internet Mail Access Protocol). IMAP mail servers manage and store copies of your mail on a remote server so you can access them from any computer in the world. IMAP is a good choice if you need to check your mail from many different computers.

The other common type of mail server uses an Internet standard called **POP** (Post Office Protocol). POP servers usually erase your email from their hard disks as soon as you've picked it up. POP is a good choice if you always use the same computer to manage your email.

*Through your .Mac Mail account, you can also **check other POP accounts** you may have!*

1. *Open your .Mac Mail.*

2. *Click the "Preferences" icon.*

3. *Click the "Accounts" tab, if it isn't showing already.*

4. *Fill in the information in the section called "Check other POP mail.*

An important advantage of web-based email

When you're at home and you send email, it gets delivered without a problem. That's because your Mail preferences include your Internet service provider's **SMTP address**—the *outgoing* mail address (*smtp.providername.net* or something similar).

To send outgoing email, it must be sent via your ISP's SMTP address, because that's who you're paying for Internet services. When you're traveling and using other connections, such as a Wi-Fi hotspot at Starbucks, you're connected through some other provider. So when you compose an email message and click

"Send," you receive a response that says your mail is not deliverable. Web-based email is one solution to that problem. When you log in to your .Mac account, you can send email because .Mac has its own SMTP address.

An alternative solution (if you don't want to limit yourself to web-mail) is to subscribe to an SMTP service, such as **SMTP.com.** For a small fee you can register a computer with SMTP.com and your mail is delivered through their service. If you don't mind paying a fee for the convenience, this enables you to do your email tasks while on the go just as if you were at home, without logging in to .Mac. See pages 156–157 for simple instructions about how to change Mail's SMTP setting to "smtp.com," and enjoy being able to effortlessly send email from your laptop, no matter where you're connected.

Start using .Mac Mail

You can use .Mac Mail in any browser on any kind of computer.

The sidebar on the .Mac page shows your .Mac Mail account and how many messages are in your inbox.

1. Go to www.mac.com.

2. Click the "Mail" link in the top navigation bar (circled below).

3. Log in to your .Mac account with your member name and password.

4. Your personal .Mac Mail page opens, as shown below.

   From this web page (and other linked pages) you can perform all your email tasks just like at home, even if you happen to be in Kathmandu.

Below are brief explanations of each button on the web-mail page. If you want excessively detailed information, please see our other book, *Cool Mac Apps.*

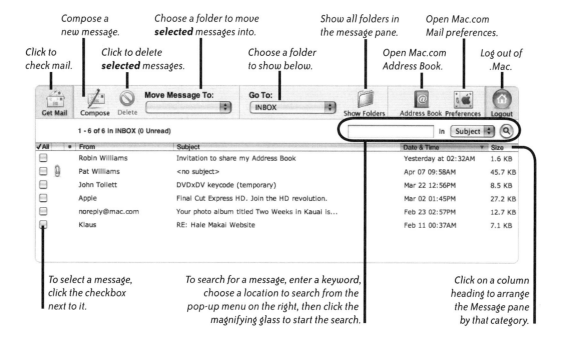

Compose a new message.

Choose a folder to move **selected** messages into.

Show all folders in the message pane.

Open Mac.com Mail preferences.

Click to check mail.

Click to delete **selected** messages.

Choose a folder to show below.

Open Mac.com Address Book.

Log out of .Mac.

To select a message, click the checkbox next to it.

To search for a message, enter a keyword, choose a location to search from the pop-up menu on the right, then click the magnifying glass to start the search.

Click on a column heading to arrange the Message pane by that category.

To get your mail and read it:

1. Click "Get Mail" in the toolbar. Messages open in the "Inbox" pane.
2. Single-click on a message in the list to open it in your browser.
3. To read another message, either click an up or down arrow, or click the "Mail" icon to go back to your Inbox.

To compose and send a message:

1. Click the "Compose" icon in the toolbar to write a new message.

2. Type an email address in the "To" field.

    To send the same message to more than one person, type other addresses in the same field with commas after each email address. **Or** put one or more addresses in the "Cc" (Carbon copy) field.

3. Type a subject line that will not be confused for junk mail!

    For instance, don't use "Hi!" or "Sorry I missed you" or "Your loan has been approved." Type a subject that will make it clear to the recipient what your message is about, that it pertains specifically to that person, or that it is certainly from you.

4. If you want to **check your spelling,** click the "Spell Check" icon in the toolbar. It will find misspelled words and offer alternative spellings in multiple languages. When you're finished, click the "Edit" button to return to the message window.

    Or try this trick: Control-click (or right-click) on any word whose spelling you're not sure of. A little menu pops up with spelling options. This method doesn't switch you to a different window, as the above Spell Check option does.

5. Click the "Send" icon in the toolbar (circled below).

Click here to save an unfinished message as a draft. Later you can open the Drafts folder (click the "Show Folders" icon in the Mail toolbar), finish the letter, and send it.

Add up to ten email addresses to the "Quick Addresses" pop-up menu (see the next page), then choose one to automatically address your message.

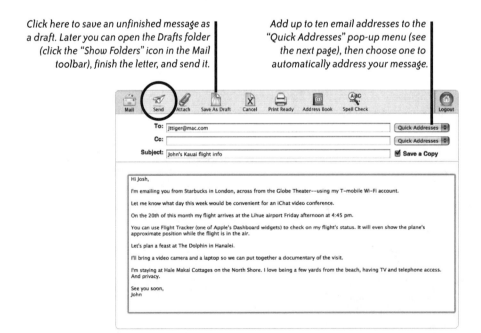

.Mac Address Book

The .Mac Address Book is similar to the Address Book on your computer. You can synchronize the Address Book information on your Mac (see page 77) with the .Mac online Address Book, making your contact information accessible from any Internet-connected computer.

Open Address Book

There are two different links to access your Address Book information while you're in .Mac Mail on the web. Each link provides slightly different options, similar to the differences on your Mac between the Address Book application and the Address Book link found in the Mail application.

To open the actual Address Book:

Click the "Address Book" link in the navigation bar or Mail toolbar (circled below). The navigation bar link is available no matter which page of Mac.com you're working in. These links open the actual Address Book where you can add records, edit, and add names to your "Quick Address" menu (see below).

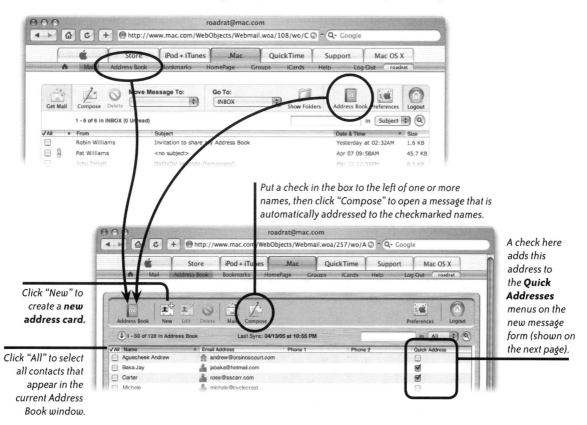

Put a check in the box to the left of one or more names, then click "Compose" to open a message that is automatically addressed to the checkmarked names.

A check here adds this address to the **Quick Addresses** menus on the new message form (shown on the next page).

Click "New" to create a **new address card**.

Click "All" to select all contacts that appear in the current Address Book window.

To show addresses from Address Book:

Click the "Compose" icon in the .Mac Mail toolbar to open a new message pane (below). In the new message pane, click the Address Book icon in the toolbar to access your Address Book data. You cannot add or edit address records here.

*This is a **new message** pane. This Address Book link does not open the actual Address Book, as on the previous page— it just opens your list of addresses.*

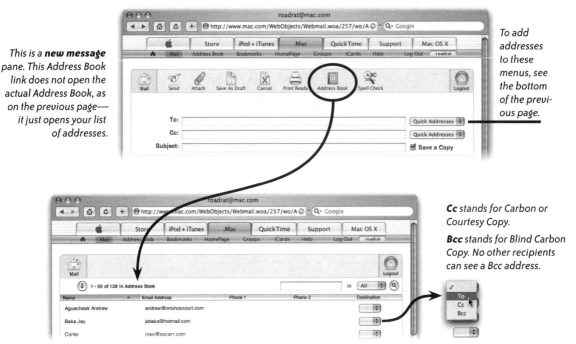

To add addresses to these menus, see the bottom of the previous page.

Cc stands for Carbon or Courtesy Copy.

Bcc stands for Blind Carbon Copy. No other recipients can see a Bcc address.

To address mail from the list:

In the "Destination" column, choose the address field in which you want that person's address to appear (To, Cc, or Bcc). At the bottom of the list, click the "Apply" button to return to the new message. The recipients' email addresses are automatically entered into the various address fields that you designated in the Destination menus.

When I click "Apply," these three people will be automatically added to these designated address fields in the new message.

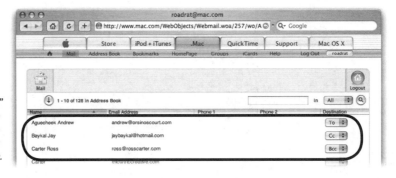

Synchronize your Address Book to .Mac

Using **iSync** (explained in greater detail on pages 65–70), you can synchro-nize the Address Book information on your main computer to your .Mac Address Book so you always have access to current contact information, no matter where you are in the world.

The default in your .Mac Address Book preferences is checked on to allow for synchronization (as shown below). If for some reason you don't want it to sync, or perhaps it didn't work, check these preferences to make sure it's turned on or off according to your need.

If the box is unchecked, the .Mac Address Book will not sync; as soon as you check the box, it will immediately sync and update your contact list.

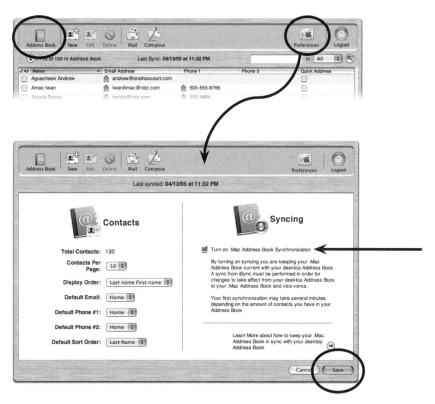

.Mac Bookmarks

When you're away from your home or office without your laptop, you may need to jump on a friend's computer or visit an Internet cafe to look up some important information that you previously bookmarked in Safari on your own computer. Most people wouldn't have access—on an Internet cafe PC, for instance—to their own bookmarks. But you're a Road Warrior, right?

Sync your Safari bookmarks

To use your Safari bookmarks on a strange computer, you need to synchronize your existing bookmarks to your .Mac account before you leave home. It might be helpful to do a little bit of housekeeping and organization of your bookmarks before you sync—now's a good time to delete bookmarks that you never use and organize the bookmarks into folders so it's easier to find them.

Once you've done that, **see pages 65–70 to synchronize the bookmarks,** which sends them to your .Mac account. Then read the rest of this section to learn how to access and use them while on someone else's computer.

Access your bookmarks on a strange computer

From almost any computer, you can go to your .Mac account in a browser and use the Safari bookmarks you set up on your own Mac.

1. Go to www.mac.com, then click "Bookmarks" in the navigation bar (circled below).

2. Type your member name and password, then click "Login."

3. You'll probably see the window shown here, unless you have recently already chosen an option. (If you have, the page shown in Step 4 opens automatically.)

   When you click OK, the Safari bookmarks on your computer are copied to the .Mac server.

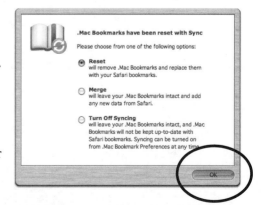

4. When the synchronization is finished, a page opens with "Welcome to .Mac Bookmarks." Click the "Open Bookmarks" button.

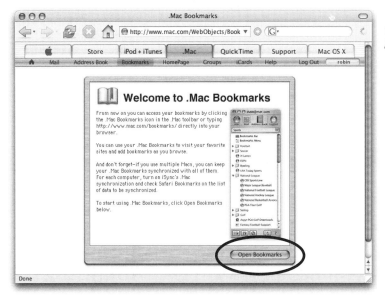

This is the Mozilla Firefox browser.

5. The .Mac Bookmarks window that opens contains a copy of your bookmarks, organized the same as on your computer.

▼ From the pop-up menu at the top of the little window, choose a particular collection (a folder) of bookmarks to display, such as "Bookmarks Menu," shown below-left. Or choose "Bookmarks Bar," shown below-right, and have access to your most favorites!

Tip: If you don't see your updated bookmarks, click the lightswitch icon at the bottom of the pane (shown below) to open the preferences.

Check the box to "Turn on .Mac Bookmarks Synchronization."

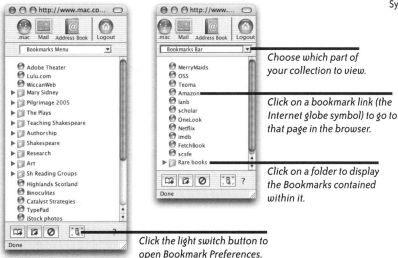

Choose which part of your collection to view.

Click on a bookmark link (the Internet globe symbol) to go to that page in the browser.

Click on a folder to display the Bookmarks contained within it.

Click the light switch button to open Bookmark Preferences.

Managing .Mac bookmarks

With the Bookmarks window open on the Desktop, you can add bookmarks, delete them, or create a new folder in which to store bookmarks. When you sync your bookmarks again, you can merge these new changes with the existing bookmarks on your main Mac.

Add bookmarks

When you're at another computer and you find a web site that you want to bookmark, don't scribble the address on a piece of scrap paper that you'll lose—bookmark it.

To add a bookmark in .Mac:

1. Open .Mac Bookmarks (as explained on the previous pages).

2. Click the bookmark-plus button (circled below-left). A new pane slides up into view (below-right).

3. Type a name for the bookmark and its address in the text fields. You don't have to include "http://" as part of the address.

4. From the "Add Bookmark To" pop-up menu in the lower section, choose a folder or area (such as the Bookmarks Bar or Menu) in which to store the bookmark.

5. Click the "Add" button (circled below-right).

6. To close the bottom pane, click the bookmark-plus button again.

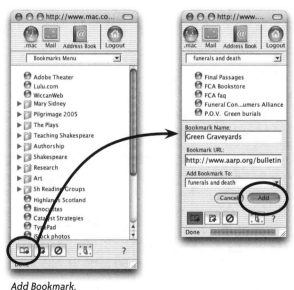

Add Bookmark.

Add folders

You may want to add new folders to keep your new bookmarks organized.

To add a folder to your bookmark collection:

1. Click the folder-plus button (circled below-left). A new pane slides up into view (below-right).

2. Type a name for the folder in the text field. From the pop-up menu right below that field, choose a folder to put the new folder in.

3. Click the "Add" button. The new folder now appears in the pop-up menu when choosing a folder for bookmarks or folders.

4. To close the pane, click the folder-plus button again.

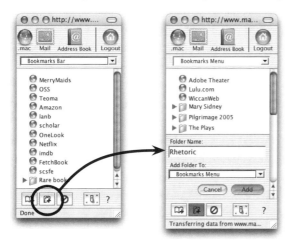

Delete bookmarks

Delete any bookmarks from this list. Later you can choose whether to have the deletions synced with your main Mac.

To delete a bookmark:

1. From the pop-up menu at the top of the window, choose the folder that contains the bookmark you want to delete.

2. Click the delete-selection button (circled below-right). A gray circle-X appears next to every item in the list.

3. Click the circle-X next to the bookmark or folder you want to delete. It turns black.

4. Click the "Delete" button to delete the selected bookmark.

5. Click the delete-selection button again to clear all of the Xs.

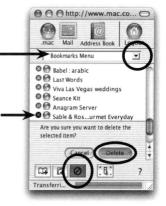

Create a .Mac Group

While on the go, you may want to keep in touch with an entire group of people—pals, family, co-workers, other people on the road. If you have a .Mac account and 45 megabytes of available iDisk space, you can create a Group that's like a home base for the entire gang. The features are amazing.

Membership to a .Mac Group is by invitation only, and you can have as many as 999 people in a group. Even though other members can refer new people to the group, as the owner you have control over who's allowed in. Members can share files, post messages, movies, photos, create their own pages, and even share a group calendar.

Non-.Mac members, including PC users, can join and participate in a .Mac Group by signing up for the sixty-day .Mac trial memberships. After the trial memberships expire, the member names are still valid and they still have access to the Group page and to the iDisk features.

To create and use a Group page:

1. Log in to your .Mac account at www.mac.com.

2. Click the "Groups" link at the top of the Mac.com page, shown below.

3. Click "Create a group" on the .Mac Groups page.

4. Fill out the short Group setup form, then click "Submit."

5. When the new Group page opens, click the "Invite" link to send email invitations to people who are invited to join the group.

When a recipient gets an invitation (above) and clicks "Join group," his browser opens to the .Mac Groups page. If he is not a .Mac member, he will be asked to sign up for a trial membership and will be given an account name. All members of the Group can access their Group page at any time by clicking the "Groups" link in the navigation bar (circled above).

6. **To post a message to the Group page,** click the "Compose" link at the top of the "Messages" window.

   Group members can also post messages without logging in to .Mac: Just send an email to the group address (YourGroupName@groups.mac.com).

A published Group page is shown below. You can create as many Groups as you want, as long as your .Mac account has enough iDisk space to allocate 45 megabytes to each Group (you can allocate more per individual group). There's a lot more to a Group than meets the eye; see the following pages.

To open your Group page, go to Mac.com, click the "Groups" button, then log in with your member name and password.

If you are the owner and logged in to edit, you will have the options shown below. Plus you can delete messages and cancel memberships.

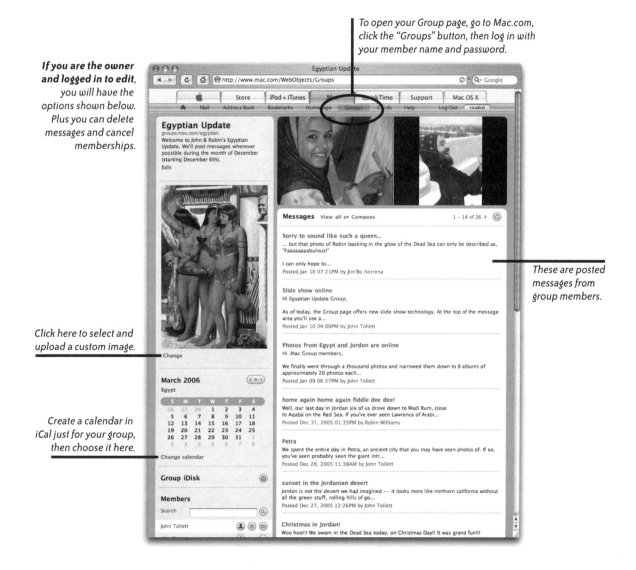

These are posted messages from group members.

Click here to select and upload a custom image.

Create a calendar in iCal just for your group, then choose it here.

Members can **add photos to the slideshow.** Hover your mouse at the bottom of the photo, then click "Add photos" when it appears.

The Group leader can create an **iCal calendar** with important dates, notes, to-do lists, rendezvous messages, etc. When Mac members **subscribe** to the calendar, the information is automatically added to their iCals (as read-only).

If a Group member has chosen to display a **profile,** she will have these icons. **To change this info,** click the "Group Preferences" link at the bottom of this page.

Group members can click either the little "www" round link or "Add." They will go straight to HomePage where they can **build a small web site** that will be hosted in the Group iDisk space and linked here.

Group members can click "Edit" and **add links** that they want to share.

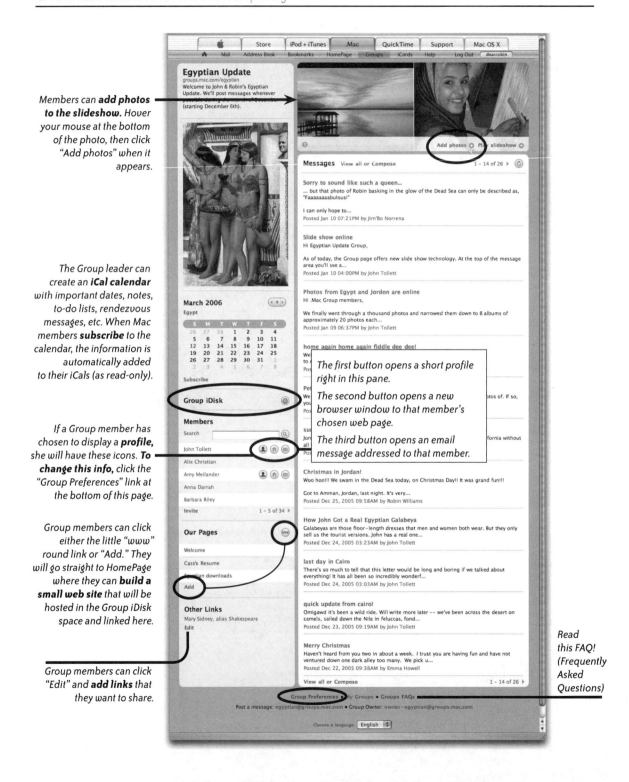

The first button opens a short profile right in this pane.

The second button opens a new browser window to that member's chosen web page.

The third button opens an email message addressed to that member.

Read this FAQ! (Frequently Asked Questions)

The Group iDisk

This is really remarkable. Circled on the opposite page is "Group iDisk" and a little round button. This is the Group's iDisk, which is 30 megabytes of allocated space on Apple's server specifically for this Group (it's taken out of the owner's iDisk allotment). Every Group member has access to this iDisk, even PC users and people whose .Mac trial memberships have expired.

To open the Group iDisk on the web, click the little Group iDisk button and the window shown below appears. Members can click the "Upload" button to find and upload files from their computers. Or anyone in the Group can download a file from any folder to her computer. Images, instead of being automatically downloaded, appear in a browser window.

Tip: You might want to remind members that the files they upload all take up space on the Group iDisk, so make sure they are appropriately sized.

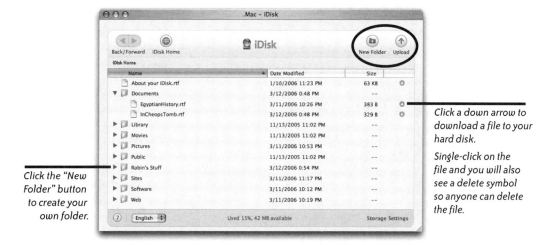

Click the "New Folder" button to create your own folder.

Click a down arrow to download a file to your hard disk.

Single-click on the file and you will also see a delete symbol so anyone can delete the file.

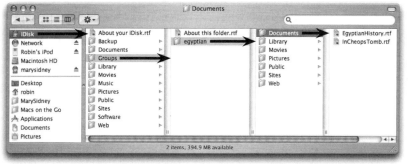

Put files into the Group iDisk from your own hard disk (if you're a .Mac member): Open your own iDisk (see page 60). Open the Groups folder, then the folder with the name of the Group. Drag files into those folders (except the Library folder).

See page 62 on how to save a file from any application on your Mac directly into the Group iDisk.

.Mac Slides

With a .Mac membership, .Mac Slides lets you publish a slideshow to your iDisk (storage space on Apple's servers). Anyone using a Mac (Mac OS X version 10.2 or later) can *subscribe* to the slideshow. It gets downloaded as a screen saver to his or her own computer—another unique and easy way to keep in touch while you're on the go. Whenever you change the images in your published slideshow, the subscribers' screen savers change. People back at home or the office can be surprised daily with your new show.

To create a .Mac slideshow to use as a screen saver:

1. Open iPhoto and make sure you're connected to the Internet.

2. Select an album of photos in the "Source" pane that you want to use for the .Mac slideshow.

   Or select individual photos from the iPhoto Library or from any album (Command-click to select multiple photos).

.Mac Slides

3. Click the ".Mac Slides" button (shown to the left) at the bottom of the window. **Or** from the Share menu, choose ".Mac Slides."

4. A message window opens (shown below). Click the "Publish" button.

When you publish a .Mac slideshow, it replaces any other slideshow you may have previously published to that .Mac account name.

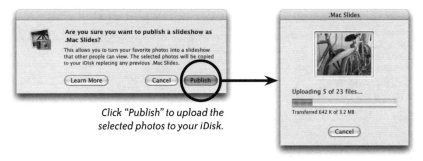

Click "Publish" to upload the selected photos to your iDisk.

5. After your photos have been uploaded to your iDisk, click the "Announce Slideshow" button (circled, to the right) to send an email announcement: An automatically generated email opens that contains instructions for viewing your .Mac slideshow. Address the email, then click "Send."

Subscribe to a slideshow screen saver

When you subscribe to a .Mac slideshow, your Mac will check the published slideshow regularly. When the publisher of the slideshow changes the photos, your Mac will go get the new ones automatically. Thus the subscriber will be continually surprised by the new images in the screen saver!

It's not a good idea to subscribe to a slideshow if you're using a dial-up connection!

To subscribe to a .Mac slideshow as a screen saver:

1. Make sure you are connected to the Internet.

2. From the Apple menu, choose "System Preferences...," or click the System Preferences icon in the Doc. Then click the "Desktop & Screen Saver" icon.

3. Click the "Screen Saver" tab (shown circled, below)

4. In the "Screen Savers" list on the left side of the dialog box, choose ".Mac."

5. Click the "Options" button. In the text field, type the .Mac member name of the person to whose slideshow you want to subscribe. You don't have to type "@mac.com."

6. Place a checkmark next to the "Display Options" you want. Click OK.

7. Now click the "Options" button again. You'll see the .Mac member name in the list of slideshows. Uncheck the box to the "Public Slide Show," then click OK.

8. Click the "Test" button to see how it looks; click to stop the test. Set the duration slider for the timing of your screen saver, then close the window.

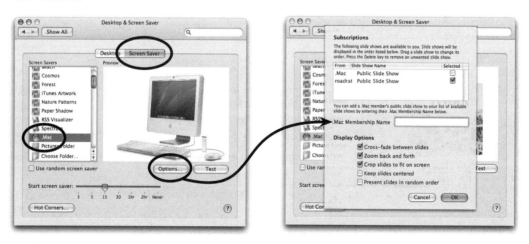

iWeb Blog and Photos

Staying in contact while you're on the go is easy if you have a .Mac account and iLife '06 (or later). With iWeb (included in iLife '06) you can keep co-workers or family up to date with a blog, or publish a web site of your recent photos from iPhoto. You can also create and publish podcasts from your laptop. We don't cover everything in this short introduction, but the Help files are great and there are tutorials on Apple's web site for greater detail.

Your blog address, after you publish it, will be web.mac.com/yourMacID.

To create and publish a blog on iWeb:

1. Open iWeb. The first thing it asks you to do is choose a template design, on the left, and then a page from that design, on the right. **Choose the "Welcome" page,** even though you're going to make a blog! If you don't, you will have a very lengthy web address instead of the one above.

If you want a lot of interaction and file-sharing between people, you might want to consider a private .Mac Group. See pages 82–85.

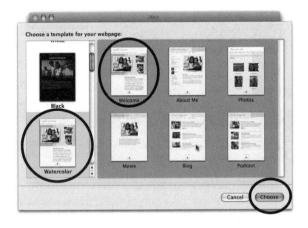

2. See pages 92–93 for the basics of how to customize the Welcome page, as well as all other pages. For now, let's add a blog page.

3. To make the blog page, click the **+** sign at the bottom-left of the pane.

4. You get the same template pane shown above. This time, double-click the "Blog" template page.

5. Now in the "Site Organizer" pane on the left side of iWeb (circled on the opposite page), you see three pages for the blog.

    Blog. This is the page that your visitors will see. See the next page.

    Entries. This is what you click on to get the page where you will type in your blog entry. See the next page.

    Archive. iWeb sets this all up for you. All you need to do is edit the placeholder text and then leave it alone.

6. In the Site Organizer, single-click on the "Blog" page to display it.

   Double-click the title at the top of the page and **rename** it.

   Double-click the "Welcome" placeholder text and **write your own.**

   Click the "Media" button at the bottom of the window to access your iPhoto collection. Drag an image from there (see an illustration of the process on page 92) and drop it on the placeholder photo in the welcome area to **replace the photo.**

These links work when the site is uploaded. While working in iWeb, use the Site Organizer to choose pages.

7. Now single-click the "Entries" page in the Site Organizer. This is where you will make your regular blog entries.

   For your first blog, double-click the existing text and replace it with your own.

   To make a new entry, click the "Add Entry" button.

   To delete an entry, select its title in the upper portion, then click the "Delete Entry" button.

8. **To publish your blog,** click the "Publish" button at the bottom of the window. You will not be asked where to put it—the pages just go. When they are uploaded, you will get a message with a link to "Visit Site Now."

   It's that easy!

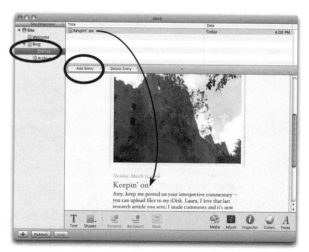

Page icons in the Site Organizer are red until you publish them. See page 93.

Create a photo album and publish it to the web

iPhoto works with iWeb to help you publish collections of your photos on your iWeb site. We have to assume you know the basics of getting your photos into iPhoto and using its Library. (If not, see *Cool Mac Apps* or the iPhoto Help menu.)

To create a new album and publish it:

Tip: If you don't want to create an album, iWeb can import a collection of selected individual photos from the Library or from any existing album.

1. In iPhoto, click the New Album button (the plus sign) in the lower-left corner of the iPhoto window. Name the album (this will also be the name of the link on the web page), and click "Create." The new album appears in the "Source" pane on the left.

2. From the iPhoto Library, drag the photos into the album that you want to put on the web site.

3. Single-click that new album in the Source pane to select it.

4. Make sure you're connected to the Internet, then click the "iWeb" icon in the iPhoto toolbar (circled below). From the pop-up menu that opens (shown below), choose "Photo Page."

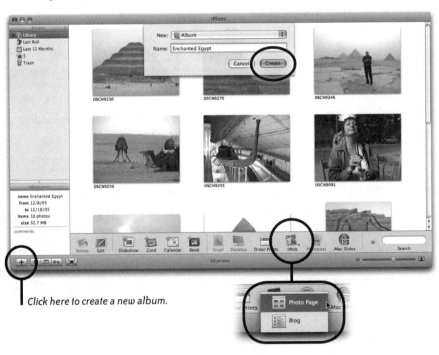

Click here to create a new album.

Note: If you choose the "Blog" option, iWeb assigns each photo (with its title) to a separate blog entry, ready for you to edit. If you have a blog page prepared, it goes on that page. If you have more than one blog in iWeb, it asks which one you want to use.

If you already have an iWeb site built (or started), this process will add a "Photos" page to your existing site.

If you don't have an iWeb site started, this process will make you one!

Now you're in iWeb:

5. In the iWeb window that opens, a sheet drops down (right) so you can choose a template. First choose a graphic style from the left column, then click the "Photos" template on the right.

6. Click "Choose."

7. iWeb imports the photos in the album you created and displays them on the iWeb template page, as shown below.

    If you already have a site in iWeb, the Photos page will be added to it and a link placed on your Welcome page.

    If you have more than one site, drag the Photos page to any site you like.

    If you have not yet made a site, iWeb creates two pages for you: the Photos page (here named "Enchanted Egypt" because that was the name of my album) and a "Welcome" page.

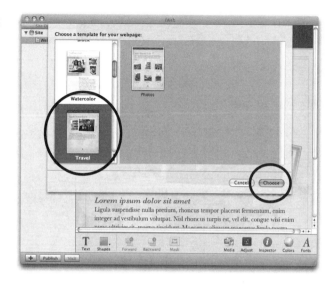

8. The text on all iWeb pages is editable: Double-click a text box to select the placeholder text, then type your own narrative. Double-click on a photo, then drag to reposition it within the border. Double-click on a photo caption to highlight it, then type a new caption.

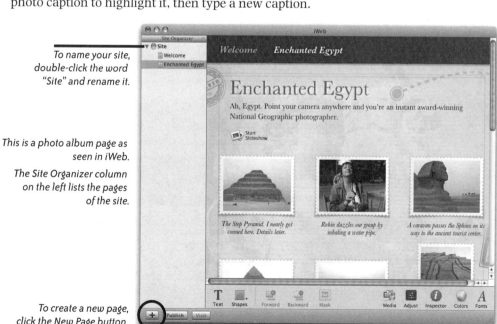

To name your site, double-click the word "Site" and rename it.

This is a photo album page as seen in iWeb.

The Site Organizer column on the left lists the pages of the site.

To create a new page, click the New Page button.

Reminder: Don't forget to save your files along the way!

9. **To edit the Welcome page,** click the "Welcome" item in the Site Organizer pane on the left to display the page. Double-click the placeholder text and type your own text for headlines and body copy.

10. **To replace the placeholder photos** in the layout with your own photos, click the "Media" icon in the toolbar; this opens the Media Browser (below-right). Drag photos from the Media Browser to the placeholder photos on the iWeb page.

   Or drag a photo from any window or folder on your computer.

To change the cropping or position of a photo, double-click to select it, then drag the image to a new position within the mask.

Click "Photos" to show iPhoto's Library and albums.

Media Browser.

Click "Publish" to upload the site files to your iDisk and publish the site to the web.

Click to open the Media Browser.

11. When you finish customizing the iWeb pages, save the file once again. Click "Publish" in the bottom-left corner. After the files have uploaded to your .Mac iDisk storage, a sheet drops down to notify you that the site is published. Choose your option.

A published iWeb site's address has a format of **web.mac.com/yourMacID.**

If you create more than one site, add the specific site name to the end of the above address to go to it.

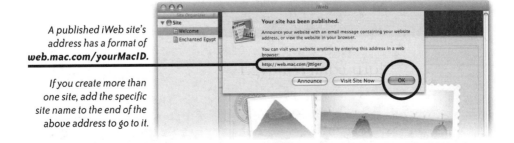

The iWeb tools

The iWeb toolbar contains tools and palettes that give you an amazing amount of control over the appearance iWeb page templates.

To create this page element, I chose a shape from the Shapes pop-up menu. I added text with the Text tool. I added drop shadows to the text and the balloon shape using the Graphic Inspector (shown below).

 Text tool. This is automatically activated when you select a place-holder text box. To add text to a shape, double-click inside the shape with the Text tool (right).

 Shapes tool. This provides a pop-up menu of ready-made shapes you can add to the page layout. You can resize or tilt the shapes.

 Forward and **Backward.** Click these tools to bring *selected* items forward or move them behind other items on the page.

 Unmask. To remove the mask around a photo and show the entire, uncropped image, select the photo, then click **Unmask**.

 Media. Click to open and close the **Media Browser** (shown on the previous page). From the Media Browser, you can select audio from iTunes or GarageBand, photos from iPhoto, and your own movies from your Movies folder or from iTunes to add to iWeb pages.

 Adjust. To adjust the appearance of a photo, select the photo, then click **Adjust**. The palette contains controls for brightness, contrast, saturation, sharpness, exposure, and more.

The Inspector palette contains seven different Inspectors in the toolbar.

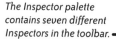

 Inspector. Click to open the Inspector palette (right). The seven Inspectors in the toolbar (across the top) give you control over all aspects of the page and site design, including drop shadows, hyperlinks, rotation, size, and orientation of images, text attributes, page size and background, site information, and more.

 Colors. This palette works with other Inspectors to control color of backgrounds, text, fills, and strokes.

 Fonts. Click to open the Font palette and choose or change the font used in headlines, captions, and body text. You can safely use any font in your list.

Blue or red page icons

The pages in the Site Organizer are color-coded.

A blue page has been published, and no changes have been made to the page since it was published.

A red page has either not been published, or its most recent changes have not been published.

Pages in the Site Organizer.

Publish a movie to iWeb

For detailed directions on how to use iMovie, please see Cool Mac Apps *by John Tollett and Robin Williams.*

For quick help, check the iMovie Help menu.

The Apple site has tutorials.

With a .Mac account, iMovie, and iWeb, you can easily publish a movie (or a few clips from a movie) while on the go. iWeb creates a web page and uploads the page and the movie (or selected clips) to your iDisk and publishes it on the Internet for others to see. All they have to do is visit your iWeb site.

If folks enjoy seeing photos of your travels before you even get home, just wait until they see movies of you on the beach while you're still in Madagascar.

To publish a movie:

1. Import video from a digital video camera into iMovie.

   If you haven't taken the time to edit your footage, just drag a few short clips from the Clips pane to the timeline. Publishing a few selected clips instead of a whole movie conserves space on your iDisk, and the short clips upload to your iDisk much faster.

   To publish only certain clips of a movie, select the clips you want in the timeline: Shift-click to select contiguous clips; Command-click to select non-contiguous clips.

Tip: If you have a clip already, put it in your Movies folder in your Home folder. Then open the Media drawer in iWeb and drag the movie onto a Movie template page.

2. From the Share menu in the menu bar, choose "Share...." Then:

   Click the "iWeb" icon in the sheet's toolbar (circled below).

   Check the button to "Share for web."

   Check "Share selected clips only" (unless you want to share the entire movie).

   Click the "Share" button.

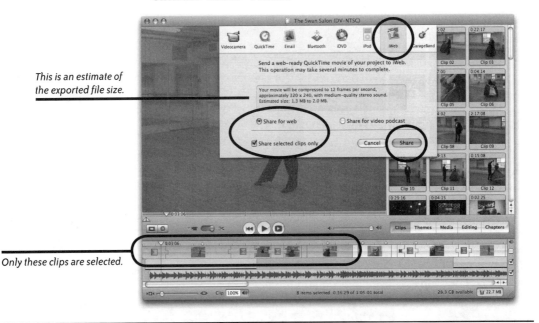

This is an estimate of the exported file size.

Only these clips are selected.

3. iMovie compresses the movie—this may take a few minutes—
then launches iWeb.

4. In the iWeb window that opens, choose a template style from the left
pane. A "Movie" page using the selected style is automatically selected.
Click the "Choose" button (circled below).

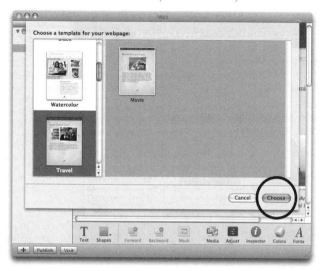

Tip: If you don't have a site already, make
sure you add a "Welcome" template page!
If you don't, you will have a very lengthy
web address instead of the succinct one
of web.mac.com/YourMemberName.

5. The iWeb page opens with
your movie placed on the page.

Notice that iWeb has created a
new page in the Site Organizer
(the left column), named for
your movie.

On the page, double-click the
placeholder body text and
replace it with text of your
own.

When you're satisfied, click
the "Publish" button.

When your page is published,
a notice appears with a web
address that you can email
to family, friends, and movie
producers.

Photocasting

Another way to share photos while on the go is Photocasting. Photocasting publishes iPhoto albums to your .Mac iDisk so other iPhoto 6 (or later) users can *subscribe* to them.

A subscriber views a Photocast in iPhoto, just as they would any other album of their own. In iPhoto preferences, a subscriber can determine how often iPhoto checks the Photocast for new images—hourly, daily, weekly, or manually.

When you subscribe to a Photocast, copies of the photos are downloaded to your computer to be used however you want—for web pages, print projects, or just viewing.

To publish a Photocast, **you must have** a .Mac membership, be running Mac OS X version 10.4.4 or later, and using iPhoto 6. **Subscribers must be running** Mac OS X version 10.4.4, *but they don't need* a .Mac membership or iPhoto 6 (they can view the Photocast in Safari).

To Photocast an album:

1. Open iPhoto. From the Source list, choose an album to publish.

2. Click the "Photocast" icon in the iPhoto toolbar (below-right). **Or** from the Share menu in the menu bar, choose "Photocast."

3. In the sheet that drops down, choose a photo size from the pop-up menu.

4. If you want changes to the Photocast album to automatically update on your iDisk, choose "Automatically update when album changes."

5. To add password protection, check "Require name and password," then type a name and password in the text fields.

6. Click "Publish." The photos are uploaded to your iDisk. When the upload is complete, an alert window tells you the address (URL) of your published album (below).

The address of your Photocast is shown here.

Egypt & Jordan

A published Photocast album in your iPhoto Source list.

Egypt & Jordan

A subscribed Photocast album in a subscriber's iPhoto Source list.

7. Click "Announce Photocast" (above) to create an email that contains the Photocast address and instructions to click the address to subscribe to the Photocast. Subscribers who don't have iPhoto 6 can copy and paste the Photocast address into Safari.

   If you set a password, use this email to tell the subscribers what the name and password is.

8. Click OK.

When a potential subscriber receives your email announcing the Photocast and clicks the link in the email, iPhoto opens (if the subscriber has iPhoto 6) and downloads the photos. A sheet drops down from the iPhoto title bar asking if they're sure they want to subscribe (shown on the right). If you set a password for the Photocast, a visitor will be asked to enter it in the fields provided.

When you make changes to the Photocast album on your Mac, the change is automatically uploaded to your iDisk. Subscribers can click the Refresh icon next to the Photocast album in the Source list to check for updates.

Backup (the application)

When you're on the go and working on your laptop, it's important to back up important files—but you may not be traveling with an external backup drive. .Mac members can log in and download an application named Backup.

Note: A friend of ours had his office burglarized. The creepy burglar not only stole his Mac, but all the backup disks of his important files. Had our friend backed up to his iDisk, he'd still have his files.

Backup can automate backup tasks for you, backing up files to CD, DVD, your hard disk, or (our Road Warrior favorite) your iDisk. Keeping a current backup of your iCal, Address Book, or an important project on iDisk means you can retrieve that information in case of emergency.

Choose your backup plans

If you haven't already downloaded Backup from the Mac.com site, log in, then download the latest version of Backup (version 3 is shown here).

1. Open the Backup application.

2. In the "Welcome to Backup" window, choose a backup plan from the list. Start with the "Personal Data & Settings" plan. This will back up your Address Book, iCal, Keychain settings, and more to your iDisk. Click "Continue."

3. The Backup window highlights your plan. Click "Back Up."

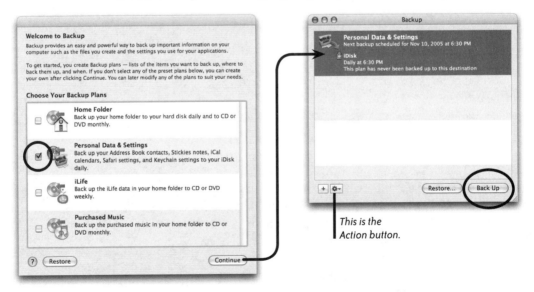

This is the Action button.

It's that simple. **To see the files that are included in the plan or to set a schedule of when the backup takes place,** double-click the item in the Backup window (above, right). The window shown at the top of the next page opens.

4. Click the "Back Up" button at the top of the window (circled, top-right) to show the "Backup Items" and the "Destination and Schedule" panes.

To add items to this plan, click the plus button (**+**) at the bottom of the "Backup Items" pane. In the sheet that drops down (below-right), choose items from the "QuickPicks" list. Click the "Files & Folders" button to select a specific file or folder. Or click the "Spotlight" button to search for a file or folder.

Since this backup plan is named "Personal Data & Settings" and because it will be backed up to your iDisk, it's best to add only QuickPicks to this plan. QuickPicks are relatively small files and they won't take up a big part of your iDisk storage. To back up large files or folders, create a custom backup plan and set the destination for another hard drive, CDs, or DVDs.

Create a custom backup plan

1. Click the Action button in the bottom-left corner of the Backup window (see the opposite page). From its menu, choose "New...." The sheet that drops down includes a "Custom" backup plan in addition to the original default backup plans (bottom-right). Select the "Custom" item, then click "Choose Plan."

2. Enter a name for the custom backup plan in the window that opens (below).

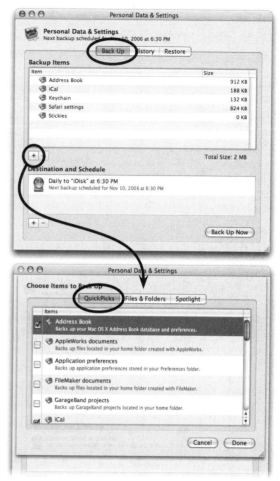

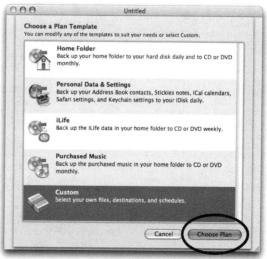

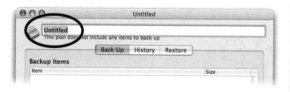

—*continued*

3. Click the plus (+) button under the "Backup Items" pane (below-left). From the sheet that drops down (below-right), select a folder or file you want to back up, then click "Done." The file or folder is added to the "Backup Items" list (below-left).

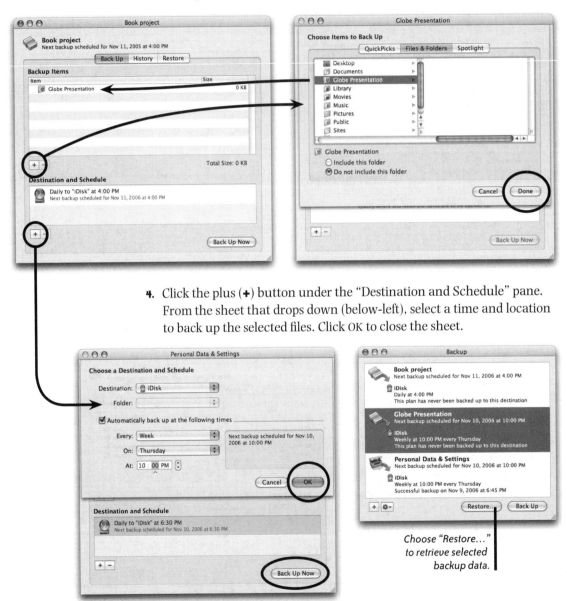

4. Click the plus (+) button under the "Destination and Schedule" pane. From the sheet that drops down (below-left), select a time and location to back up the selected files. Click OK to close the sheet.

Choose "Restore..." to retrieve selected backup data.

5. Click "Back Up Now." The new backup plan is added to the list of backup plans (above right). To manually activate a plan instead of waiting for the scheduled backup, select it, then click "Back Up."

iChat and Bonjour
for Easy Communication

iChat AV allows you to communicate with others instantly—no waiting for email to be read and answered. When you see a buddy in your Buddy List window, you can send an instant text message. With iChat it's easy (and free) to communicate with friends and associates almost anywhere in the world.

In addition to text messaging, those with iChat and broadband connections can have *audio* and *video* chats.

iChat includes **Bonjour,** an application that is similar to iChat, but you'll use it to communicate across local area networks instead of the Internet. Bonjour detects other Macs on the network and connects to them, making communication and file sharing effortless and automatic. If you have two or more computers networked, Bonjour will be one of your favorite features.

Text, Audio, or Video Chat

Tip: A .Mac member's instant messaging name includes *@mac.com*.

An AIM or AOL instant messaging name does not include @ anything.

iChat AV requires a buddy name and a computer with Mac OS X installed. The buddy name can be your .Mac account name (remember, anyone can get a trial membership for free and then keep the name), your AOL buddy name (if you have an AOL account), or an AIM (AOL Instant Messenger) buddy name that you can get, free, at the AIM web site (www. AIM.com).

The various ways to use iChat have varying requirements:

▼ **Text chat.** Text messaging needs only a low bandwidth connection, as low as a dial-up modem.

▼ **Audio chat.** An audio chat requires a broadband connection (such as cable, DSL, or Wi-Fi) and a microphone (all recent Mac laptops have built-in microphones).

▼ **Video conference.** A video conference requires a broadband connection, such as cable, DSL, or Wi-Fi. It also requires a FireWire-enabled video camera.

Apple's iSight camera, available from the Apple site is small, compact, inexpensive, and includes a built-in microphone. The MacBook Pro laptops have iSight cameras built in.

All current Apple laptops are equipped to handle audio and video chats. If you plan to chat with people on desktop computers, the desktop computer needs to be at least a G3 with a 600 MHz processor for audio or video conferencing.

An iSight camera, shown
mounted on a PowerBook screen.

Clues in your Buddy List

We have to assume that iChat is set up and functioning. Your Buddy List, shown below, gives you an instant clue as to what kind of chat you can do with that person, so you don't have to worry about all those technical specs to find out. If you don't have anyone in your Buddy List yet, see the following pages.

If you need help setting up iChat, please see Cool Mac Apps, *or the iChat Help files (from the Help menu when iChat is open), or the tutorials on the Apple.com site.*

- ▾ **No icon.** This buddy can only use text messages to chat.
- ▾ **Phone icon.** This buddy has a microphone attached or built in and can use text or audio to chat.
- ▾ **Multiple-phone icon.** This buddy has a system powerful enough to support an audio chat with more than one person.
- ▾ **Camera icon.** The buddy has a video camera attached and can use text, audio, or video to chat.
- ▾ **Multiple-camera icon.** The buddy has a big ol' machine and a multiple-person video chat is possible, as well as text and audio.

Text chat. | Video chat.
Audio chat.

Green orb. The buddy is online and you can start a chat with her.

Amber orb. The buddy is online, but his computer is idle, meaning he's probably been away from it for a bit.

Red orb. The buddy has chosen to be unavailable and doesn't want to be disturbed, even though he's online.

Tip: The ***dimmed*** buddies at the bottom of the list are offline and unavailable

To ***hide*** offline buddies, go to the View menu and uncheck "Show Offline Buddies."

Quick start

If you're set up and you've got some buddies in your list, try these tips below.

- ▾ **Double-click the buddy name** and iChat will initiate a text chat.
- ▾ **Single-click the media icon** (the phone or camera) and iChat will initiate the kind of chat indicated by the icon.
- ▾ **To initiate a specific kind of chat,** single-click on a buddy's name, then click one of the chat buttons at the bottom of the window.
- ▾ **Control-click a buddy name,** then choose a chat option from the contextual menu that opens.

Create a Buddy List

No matter what kind of chatting you plan to do (text, audio, or video), the first thing you need is a Buddy List. The Buddy List lets you see when your friends or associates are online, and with the click of a button you can start a chat or send a file.

To add someone to your Buddy List:

1. Open iChat. If you don't see your Buddy List on the screen, press Command 1 (the number "one"), **or** go to the Window menu and choose "Buddy List."

2. In the Buddy List, click the **+** button (circled below-left). A sheet containing your Address Book contacts drops down from the top of the window (below-right).

Although you see options for MSN, ICQ, and Yahoo, they don't work in iChat.

3. **If the person you want to add is in your Address Book,** select his or her name, then click the "Select Buddy" button (circled above).

   If this person's address card *includes an instant messaging name,* (as shown to the left) the name is added to your Buddy List. You're done.

   If the card *does not include an instant messaging name,* follow the steps below.

   If the person you want to add is not in your Address Book, or if their address card *does not include an instant messaging name,* click the "New Person" button (circled above).

4. A new sheet drops down, as shown on the opposite page. From the "Account Type" pop-up menu, select ".Mac" *if* the new person uses their Mac.com account for instant messaging.

   Or choose "AIM" if the new buddy uses an AOL or AIM screen name.

5. Enter the new name in the "Account Name" field.

   The Buddy List uses the entry from the First Name and Last Name fields to name the buddy in the list. If you don't enter a first or last name, the Buddy List displays the Account Name.

   Whatever you enter in this sheet is actually being added to a new card in your Address Book. Later, if you want to change a buddy's information, you can open Address Book and change it there.

   Or you can select a buddy in the Buddy List, then from the Buddies menu in the menu bar, choose "Get Info" to open an Address Book window for that buddy.

6. **To add a photo or custom icon** to a buddy's name in the list, drag an image on top of the "Buddy Icon" well, shown below-left. The photo can be a JPEG, GIF, TIFF or Photoshop file.

7. Click the "Add" button to add the new buddy to your Buddy List (and to your Address Book).

Tip: After you add a photo or image, you can choose to have the one *you* added override the one your buddy has chosen. Do this in the "Get Info" window for that buddy.

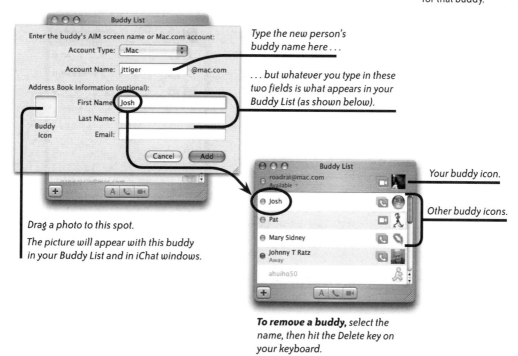

Type the new person's buddy name here . . .

. . . but whatever you type in these two fields is what appears in your Buddy List (as shown below).

Drag a photo to this spot.

The picture will appear with this buddy in your Buddy List and in iChat windows.

Your buddy icon.

Other buddy icons.

To remove a buddy, select the name, then hit the Delete key on your keyboard.

Text Chat

Text chats are quick and easy and have that email advantage of being a step back from the more personal audio and video. Make sure you're connected to the Internet before you try to chat.

Text chats are easy to start

You can have a text chat with one person or with a group of people. Each one starts in a different way; that is, you can't start a one-person chat and then add more—you must decide before you open the chat which one you want.

To start a text chat with one person:

1. Open iChat and the Buddy List (if the list is not immediately visible, choose "Buddy List" from the Window menu in the menu bar).

2. Double-click a name (not an icon) in the Buddy List; this automatically opens a text chat window. An invitation to chat is sent to the buddy.

3. Start typing in the text field at the bottom of the chat window.

   To add a smiley icon (an emoticon), click on the little smiley face in the text field and choose one. If you type an emoticon, such as ;-), it will turn into the cartoon version automatically.

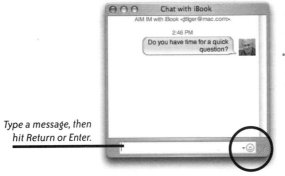

Type a message, then hit Return or Enter.

To customize the look of your chat window, use the iChat preferences (from the iChat application menu). Click on the "Messages" icon in the preferences toolbar and choose your bubble color and fonts.

To display your chat in all text, while the chat window is open, go to the View menu and choose "Show as Text."

To start a text chat with more than one person:

1. Open iChat and the Buddy List.

2. From the File menu, choose "New Chat." This opens a chat window with a drawer on the side, as shown at the top of the next page.

3. Click the **+** sign at the bottom of the drawer to get a list of the available buddies to invite to the chat. Choose as many as you want.

4. In the text field at the bottom of the iChat window, type your message. It will go to all the people you have invited. You can invite more buddies to join the chat at any time.

*This is a group text chat.
You can invite lots of people.*

Private chat rooms

You can open a private chat "room" that others can enter at any time without having to be invited. This is useful if you want to do something like call a meeting around the world and expect people to show up. You tell them what time and the name of the private room, and they join you as they can.

Naming the room: Choose a name that no one else is likely to know because anyone in the world can join your private chat room if they enter the same name! The name is not case-specific, meaning it doesn't matter if people use capital or lowercase letters. You can re-use the same name as often as you like.

To open or join a private chat room:

1. In iChat, go to the File menu and choose "Go to Chat...." This opens a little window where you type the name of the room.

2. A chat window opens. If you are the first one to type in that name, you'll be alone in the room until someone else checks in.

   If others typed the name first, you will join them in the room.

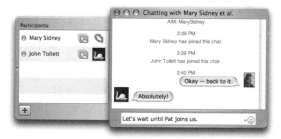

To invite someone to join the room, click the + sign and enter their instant message name.

Save transcripts of text chats

You can save a transcript of any text chat to read again later, or perhaps to document an important business conversation while you're on the road.

To save an individual chat:

1. Single-click on the chat you want to save to make it the active window.

2. From the File menu, choose "Save a Copy As...."

3. You'll be asked to name the document and choose where to store it, then click "Save." It only saves what has been typed so far; that is, if you add more to the chat, you'll have to save it again.

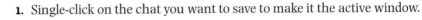

AntShannie on
2005-03-15 at 17.48

A saved iChat transcript looks like this.

To automatically save all chat transcripts:

1. From the iChat menu, choose "Preferences...."

2. Click the "Messages" button in the preferences toolbar.

3. Check the box to "Automatically save chat transcripts." This creates a new folder inside your Documents folder called "iChats." Every conversation you have in iChat will automatically be recorded and stored in this folder.

To read any saved chat:

▼ Double-click the chat file icon, wherever you stored it. The file will open in a chat window and you can scroll through it just like an active chat window.

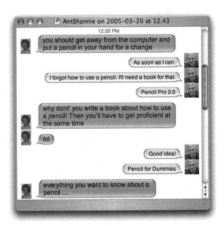

A saved iChat transcript opens as shown here, but prints as text, as shown below.

To print a chat:

1. Open a text chat.

2. From the iChat File menu, choose "Print...."

3. In the Print dialog box, click "Print." **Or** click the "Preview" button to see what it will look like, then click "Print." The chat prints as a text transcript, as shown above.

John Tollett: The fabulous, gorgeous Andrew Wyeth book been my favorite for a long long time.
antshannie: You're welcome! Sorry it didn't get ther
John Tollett: No problem. It's nice stretching out the surpr
antshannie: we've seen 2 of his exhibits. I don't mu by my tastes
John Tollett: He is amazing.

Audio Chat

You need a broadband connection (not a dial-up modem connection) to audio chat. Travelers will be pleased to know that many hotels and lodges around the world provide broadband connections. The broadband wireless connections (Wi-Fi) that many coffee shops provide also work very well for audio chats.

To start an audio chat:

1. If your buddy displays a telephone icon in the Buddy List, then you can start an audio chat: Double-click the phone icon next to her name.

2. An invitation to chat is sent to the buddy and the small window shown below opens.

3. Your buddy will hear a telephone sound ringing from her computer; she has to click the button to "Accept" the call. Start talking.

4. To add more people to your audio chat, click the **+** button to get a list of available buddies to add.

Direct your voice toward the laptop screen and its built-in microphone.

Set up for audio chats

Audio chats require almost no setup. In fact, the settings below are automatic and *you don't need to change them unless you have a problem connecting.*

1. Make sure you have a microphone connected or built in to your Mac. All current Mac laptops have built-in microphones.

2. Open iChat. From the iChat menu, choose "Preferences...," then click the "Video" icon in the toolbar.

3. From the "Microphone" pop-up menu, choose a source for audio.

   iSight Built-in. If you have an Apple iSight camera connected, choose this. If you have some other FireWire video camera connected, the camera name or model number appears in this pop-up menu.

   Internal microphone. Use the built-in microphone in your laptop.

   Line In. Use this if you have an external microphone connected to your Mac through the Line In port.

Video Chat

Free video-conferencing on your little laptop, all around the world! Robin's mother has called her for video chats in Oxford, Bermuda, London, and Amman (and regularly in Santa Fe). It's remarkably easy. If your computer is powerful enough and the broadband connection fast enough, you can video conference with four people at once.

It takes a more powerful computer and a faster Internet connection to *initiate* a video chat than it does to *participate* in one.

Set up for video chats

▼ **Connect a FireWire-enabled video camera to your Mac and turn it on.** Apple sells a great little FireWire camera called iSight for $150. The MacBook Pro laptops have a built-in camera. iSight cameras are automatically set to record.

If you already own a digital video camera with FireWire, you can use that. Make sure the videocam is in *Camera* or *Record* mode.

To start a video chat:

1. If your buddy displays a camera icon in the Buddy List, then you can start a video chat: Single-click the camera icon next to her name.

2. An invitation to chat is sent to the buddy and the small window shown below opens.

3. Your buddy will hear a telephone sound ringing from her computer; she has to click the button to "Accept" the call.

4. Start talking.

5. To add more people to your video chat, click the **+** button to get a list of available buddies to add.

Point your FireWire-enabled camera at yourself (or wherever you want) and start talking when your buddy appears in the main iChat video window.

Your image will appear in a tiny inset. You can drag this inset around in the window.

One-way video chat

Even when your buddy doesn't have a FireWire camera attached, you can still have a *one-way* video chat. You'll show up on the buddy's screen in an iChat video window and she can hear you and see you; you can hear her, but you can't see her.

To have a one-way video chat:

1. Select a buddy in your Buddy List, even if he doesn't have a camera icon next to his name.

2. From the Buddies menu, choose "Invite to One-Way Video Chat."

3. Your buddy receives a video chat invitation. When the buddy clicks the "Accept" button, you appear in an iChat window on his Desktop.

Send or Receive Files through iChat

While you're on the go, you may want to **send a picture or some important file** to someone. This technique only works if your buddy is also an iChat user; if the buddy is an AOL user, you'll have to send the file as an email attachment.

To send a file to another iChat user in your Buddy List:

1. Drag a file's icon on top of a buddy's name in the Buddy List.

2. An alert appears on your Desktop so you can cancel or send the file. Click "Send."

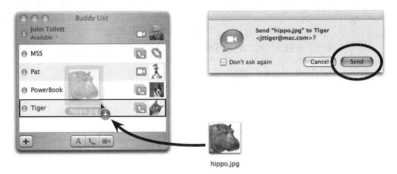

hippo.jpg

You can also send a file by dragging it into the text field while you're having a text chat. Just drop the file in the text field and hit Return. You can put text in the same field, too.

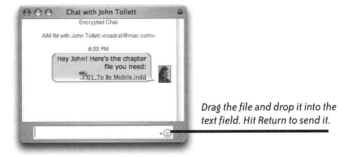

Drag the file and drop it into the text field. Hit Return to send it.

To receive a file from an iChat user:

On the recipient's computer (assuming it's an iChat user, not an AOL user), an alert appears warning of an incoming file, as shown on the next page.

1. Click anywhere in the white alert panel to transform it into the "Incoming File Transfer" window. The panel identifies the sender, file name, file type, and file size.

2. Based on the information in the "Incoming File Transfer" window, you can "Decline" the transfer, or click the "Save File" button and download it. If you save the file, it appears on your Desktop.

Tip: You can specify another location to save received files in the General pane of iChat preferences.

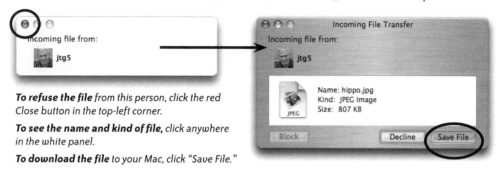

To refuse the file from this person, click the red Close button in the top-left corner.

To see the name and kind of file, click anywhere in the white panel.

To download the file to your Mac, click "Save File."

Encrypt iChat messages

For secure communications, Mac OS X version 10.4.3 or later provides the option of encrypting iChat messages between .Mac members. Both parties who are engaged in the chat must have iChat encryption turned on. When you set up iChat for the first time, encryption was probably turned on. You can check to make sure.

To enable (or disable) iChat encryption:

1. From the iChat application menu, choose "Preferences...."

2. Click the "Accounts" icon in the toolbar across the top.

3. In the Accounts pane on the left side of the window, select the account you want to secure.

4. Click the "Security" tab (circled) to show the Security settings.

5. Click the "Enable" (or "Disable") button at the bottom of the pane.

Tip: If you're in a public place with a wireless connection, such as an Internet cafe, you should quit iChat when you're not using it to safeguard your privacy and security.

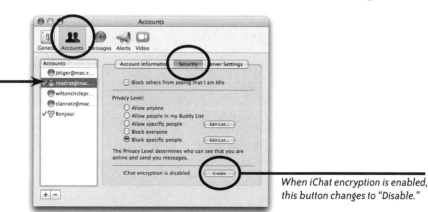

When iChat encryption is enabled, this button changes to "Disable."

Bonjour

iChat isn't just for Road Warriors who are away from home. Sometimes you need to communicate or share files with someone in your home or in the office down the hall, or you need to send files from your desktop Mac to your laptop in preparation for a business trip.

Tip: If you're in a public space with a wireless connection, such as an Internet cafe, you should quit iChat/Bonjour when you're not using it to safeguard your privacy and security.

Bonjour is the *local area network* version of iChat. If you have two or more Macs connected through a local area network (Ethernet, wireless, or a combination of both), Bonjour *automatically* detects and connects all of the computers on the local network.

You can send files or instant text messages to Bonjour buddies. You can also conduct audio or video chats with others on the local network if a microphone or digital video camera is connected to your Mac.

To use Bonjour, you don't need a .Mac account or an AIM account, as required to use iChat on the Internet. iChat (which automatically includes Bonjour) must be installed on all computers that you want to connect to, Bonjour must be turned on (see the opposite page), and the computers must be connected through some sort of network.

To set up Bonjour:

1. Open iChat.
2. Go to the Window menu and choose "Bonjour."
3. **If Bonjour is enabled**, well, there you are.

   If Bonjour is not enabled, you will be asked if you want to log in. Click "Login" and there you are.

Bonjour automatically goes about its job of detecting other iChat users on your local network, so when you're ready to chat or send files, the other user only has to be notified.

Using Bonjour

Just about everything that applies to iChat (described on the previous pages) also applies to Bonjour. Remember, iChat connects to buddies through the *Internet*, and Bonjour connects to buddies who are on your *local network*—otherwise, text chats, audio chats, video chats, and file sharing look and work the same as in iChat.

My, this looks familiar.

In fact, sometimes it's easy to lose track of which application you're using, iChat or Bonjour. To see which one you're using, look at the top of a message window for a line of gray type.

A Bonjour message window.

An iChat message window.

Bonjour account information

If you need to enable or disable Bonjour, or if you want to change any of the settings, you can do so at any time.

To change the Bonjour preferences:

1. Open iChat, then go to the iChat menu and choose "Preferences...."

2. Click the "Accounts" button in the tool bar of the preferences window.

3. Click the "Bonjour" item in the Accounts pane on the left to display its "Account Information" on the right.

4. **To turn on Bonjour,** check "Use Bonjour Instant Messaging."

   To disable Bonjour, uncheck the box.

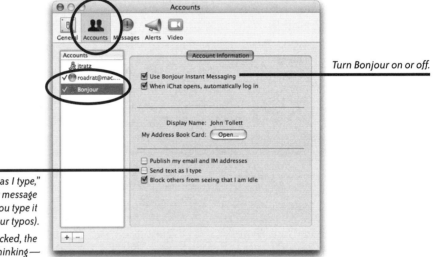

Turn Bonjour on or off.

If you check "Send text as I type," the recipient of your message will see the text as you type it (and see you fixing your typos).

If you leave this unchecked, the recipient sees you thinking— a little message cloud— until you hit Return.

iCal Calendars
for Mobile Computing

When you're on the go, you don't want to lose track of important events just because you left your calendar on the office wall. iCal helps keep track of meetings, appointments, To Do lists, birthdays, and any other important events. Color-coding makes it easy to view multiple calendars at once and instantly know if any events are overlapping. For instance, you can easily tell if your lunch meeting overlaps with a doctor's appointment, or if your afternoon trip to the Apple Store conflicts with a scheduled job interview. You can set iCal alarms to remind you an event is approaching. And, as you travel, you can switch between your current time zone and your home time zone.

But it gets even better. You can publish one or more iCal calendars on the Internet so you can access it from any computer. You can subscribe to online calendars, and other people can subscribe to your calendar. If you've set up a .Mac Group page through a .Mac account, you can link the Group page to one of your published calendars.

The iCal Window

iCal's window provides access to all calendars, views, events, and To Do lists. Color-coding makes it easy to glance at multiple calendars in the window and instantly see if there are any overlapping events. Each person in your family can have their own color-coded calendar. And you can create separate calendars for special projects, events, or interests.

Your list of calendars

The upper-left pane of the iCal window shows the **Calendars** list. The list contains calendars that you've created or to which you've subscribed. You can select any calendar in the list to show just that calendar's information (check its checkbox) in the main View pane. Select multiple calendars to show them simultaneously in iCal.

When you click one event, all events in that particular calendar are brought forward and shown in full-strength color. Events that belong to non-selected calendars have dimmed color and are sent to the back.

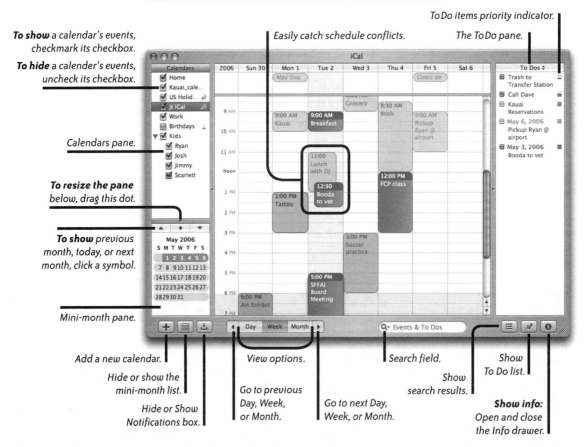

ToDo items priority indicator.

To show a calendar's events, checkmark its checkbox.

To hide a calender's events, uncheck its checkbox.

Easily catch schedule conflicts.

The To Do pane.

Calendars pane.

To resize the pane below, drag this dot.

To show previous month, today, or next month, click a symbol.

Mini-month pane.

Add a new calendar.

Hide or show the mini-month list.

Hide or Show Notifications box.

View options.

Go to previous Day, Week, or Month.

Go to next Day, Week, or Month.

Search field.

Show search results.

Show To Do list.

Show info: Open and close the Info drawer.

Choose a calendar view

The appearance of the main View pane changes according to which view option you choose: Day, Week, or Month.

Previous   Next

▼ **To choose a view,** click one of the View buttons at the bottom of the iCal window (shown on the right).

▼ **To go to the *previous* or *next* day, week, or month** in any view, click the small triangles on either side of the View buttons.

The mini-month pane

The mini-month pane lets you jump to any day, week, or month of any year.

▼ **To display a particular month** in iCal's main View pane, select the month you want to see in the mini-month list.

▼ **To scroll forward or backward in time through the mini-month calendars,** click the Up and Down triangles located at the top of the mini-month pane.

Previous   Next

Mini-month.

Return to today's date

There are several easy ways **to get back to the current date** after jumping to future dates in iCal. Do one of the following:

▼ In the mini-month pane, click the diamond-shaped symbol at the top of the list (between the up and down triangles).

▼ **Or** from the View menu, choose "Go to Today."

▼ **Or** press Command T.

The Notifications box

The Notifications box lets you know when you've received email with an iCal invitation to an event, or an email reply to an iCal event invitation that you sent. When the iCal icon in your Dock shows a red circle with a number in it, check the iCal Notifications box.

Hide or Show the Notifications box.

Change the number of days shown

To change the number of days that show in Week view, press Command Option plus any number from 1 through 7 (e.g., Command Option 3 shows three days instead of seven days). Or change the "Days per week" setting in iCal preferences.

Create a New Calendar

Keep track of the schedules of selected family, friends, or colleagues. If you share a user account on your Mac with other family members, you can view their individual calendars in iCal.

To create a new calendar, click the New Calendar button (the plus sign) in the bottom-left corner, and type a name for the new untitled calendar. Click the new calendar in the Calendars list, then click the Show Info button to open the Info drawer. Choose a color for the calendar from the pop-up color menu found in the top-right corner of the Info drawer (shown below).

To change the color of a calendar, select the calendar (click once on its name) in the Calendars list, click the Show Info button, then choose a color from the pop-up menu in the Info drawer (below-right).

To change a calendar name, double-click the name in the Calendars list, then type a new name.

Create a Calendar Group

Organize calendars by grouping similar calendars together, as shown below with the "Kids" group. If several people use your computer, each person could have a separate group for all of their personal calendars.

From the File menu, choose "New Calendar Group." Name the new group in the Calendars list, then drag individual calendars into the group by dropping them on top of the new group name. You can also create a new calendar group by Shift-clicking the New Calendar button (below-left).

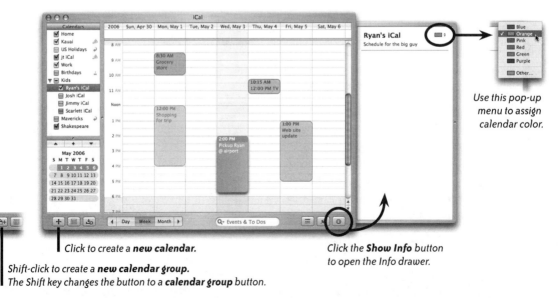

Use this pop-up menu to assign calendar color.

Click to create a **new calendar.**

Shift-click to create a **new calendar group.**
The Shift key changes the button to a **calendar group** button.

Click the **Show Info** button to open the Info drawer.

Create a New Event

Items that you enter into a calendar are called **events**. An event can be an appointment, party, reminder, all-day class, week-long seminar, or anything else that's in your schedule.

To create an event:

1. Select one of the calendars in the Calendars list. If none of the existing calendars seem appropriate for the new event you want to add, create a new calendar, as explained on the previous page.

2. In the View pane, press-and-drag vertically in the time slot in which you want to place an event.

   Or double-click the time slot where you want to place a new event. After you create the event, you can drag it to any position in the calendar. You can also drag an event's edge to change its duration.

   Or click once in a time slot, then from the File menu choose "New Event."

3. When you create a new event, the text "New Event" is already selected, so all you have to do is type a description or name for the event.

   Or click the Show Info button to open the Info drawer (shown on the right), then click on the text at the top of the drawer and type a description. Anything you type here appears in the event block in the calendar, and vice versa.

4. **Set the other options in the drawer:**

   To **repeat** this event in the calendar, click the repeat pop-up button (the small double-arrows) to open a menu containing recurrence choices.

   You can invite **attendees** to an event.

   To switch the event to another **calendar,** click the calendar pop-up button (the small double-arrows) and assign the event to another calendar.

   To set an **alarm** for the event, click the alarm pop-up button, then choose a type of alarm and how soon before the event you want the alarm to activate.

   If the event has a web site, enter the address in the **url** field so you can access it with a click.

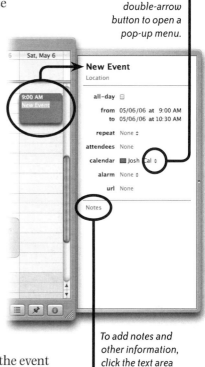

Click the small double-arrow button to open a pop-up menu.

To add notes and other information, click the text area labeled "Notes."

Create an all-day event or a multi-day event

All-day and **multi-day events** are represented by rounded rectangles that stretch the width of the event duration. In Day or Week view, they appear in a row at the top of the calendar in order to leave more room for other items in the main window and to avoid overlapping events in the main calendar area.

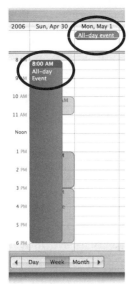

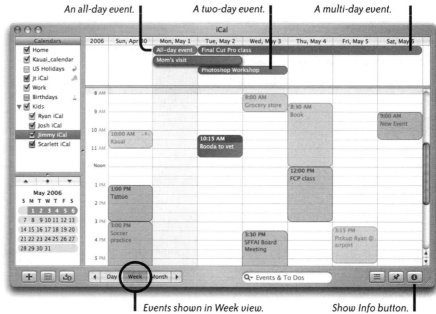

An all-day event. | A two-day event. | A multi-day event.

Events shown in Week view. | Show Info button.

In the left column above, an all-day event has been created by dragging the event's bottom edge down to an all-day duration. This technique crowds other items in the calendar.

In the right column, the same event has been designated as an all-day event in the Info drawer. This technique moves the all-day event to the top, out of the way of other events.

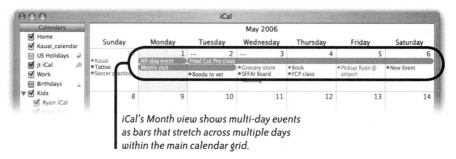

iCal's Month view shows multi-day events as bars that stretch across multiple days within the main calendar grid.

To create an all-day event:

1. Create a new event in iCal. **Or** select an existing event that you want to change to an all-day event.

2. Click the Show Info button to open the Info drawer (shown on the right).

3. Click the "all-day" checkbox.

4. Press the Return key to apply the setting.

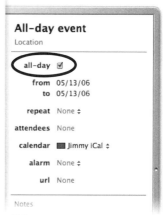

All-day event.

To create a multi-day event:

1. Create a new event (page 121). **Or** select an existing event that you want to change to a multi-day event.

2. Click the Show Info button to open the Info drawer.

3. Click the "all-day" checkbox.

4. Click the "from" and "to" values to set the event dates: Click the day, month, or year value, then press the Up or Down arrow on your keyboard to change the value. **Or** type a value to replace the highlighted value.

5. In Week view you can drag an existing event to the all-day space at the top of the calendar, then drag the event's edge to stretch across multiple days.

    To convert a multi-day event into a regular event, Control-click on the event and choose "Make Regular Event."
    Or uncheck the "all-day" checkbox in the Info drawer.

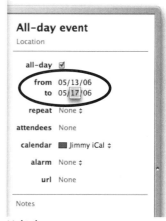

Multi-day event.

To create recurring events:

1. Click an event in iCal to select it.

2. Click the Show Info button to open the Info drawer.

3. Click the "repeat" pop-up menu (shown on the right). Choose one of the repeat options in the pop-up menu.

4. Select "Custom" from the pop-up menu if you want to make additional settings in the window shown below.

These settings are available when you select "Custom..." from the "repeat" pop-up menu.

5. Click OK (above) to apply your settings.

Repeat event.

Delete an Event

To manually delete an event, select it, then press the Delete key on your keyboard. **To delete multiple events at once,** Shift-select two or more events, then press Delete. **Or** select the event/s, go to the Edit menu, and choose "Delete."

To automatically delete events that have passed:

1. From the iCal menu, choose "Preferences…," then click the "Advanced" button (shown below).

2. Check "Delete events," then enter the number of days to keep past events.

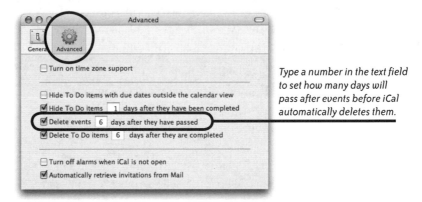

Type a number in the text field to set how many days will pass after events before iCal automatically deletes them.

An alert warns that setting this option will automatically delete events older than six days (or whatever number you designate), and asks for confirmation. Click "Yes" to delete old events.

The setting above keeps iCal from becoming cluttered with old events. However, if you want to keep a record of schedules, appointments, and events, you can uncheck the "Delete events" checkbox and let iCal permanently store your information.

iCal – 4/22/05.icbu

When you choose "Back up Database" from the File menu, the backup file looks like this.

But there are **several better ways** to protect your iCal database:

▼ From the File menu choose "Back up Database…." At a later date, if necessary, choose "Revert to Database Backup" from the File menu.

▼ Manually backup iCal files (page 136).

▼ If you have a .Mac account, use Backup (see page 136).

▼ Use iSync (Chapter 4).

For best protection, use two or more of these techniques.

Move an Event

To move an event to another day or time, drag the event to a new location in the calendar window. If the date is not visible in your current view, change to another view. For instance, in Month view you can drag an event anywhere in the month.

To move an event to another month or year:

1. Single-click the event to select it.

2. Click the Show Info button to open the Info drawer.

3. In the Info drawer, change the month, date, or year information. The event immediately jumps to the new setting's calendar location.

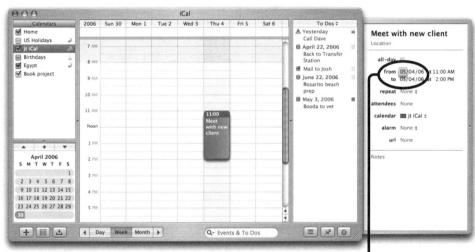

Click the month, day, or year field to select it,
then type in a new value, or use the Up and
Down arrow keys to change the value.

To move an event to another calendar:

When you move an event to a different calendar, nothing changes except the color of the item in the calendar grid (and some invisible iCal reorganization).

- ▼ **Either** Control-click the event, then choose a calendar from the pop-up menu that opens. The event will change to the color associated with the new calendar category.

- ▼ **Or** select an event, click the Show Info button, then in the Show Info drawer (above), choose a calendar from the "calendar" pop-up menu.

Change iCal's Time Zone Setting

iCal uses the time zone setting in your Date & Time preferences to set the time zone for your calendars. You can *change the time zone setting for iCal,* **or** you can change the time zone setting for *a single event,* without changing your Date & Time preferences.

If, for instance, you create an iCal event to call someone at a certain time in another time zone, you can set that event to the other person's time zone. *iCal moves the event forward or back in time in your calendar* to compensate for the time zone difference. Or if you take a trip and want to change all calendars and events in iCal to your current time zone, you can do that with a click or two.

To change the time zone setting for iCal:

1. Open iCal Preferences. In the "Advanced" pane, select "Turn on time zone support" to show a time zone setting in the top-right corner of the iCal window, and also in the Info drawer (below).

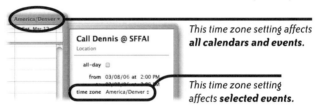

This time zone setting affects **all calendars and events.**

This time zone setting affects **selected events.**

2. Click the time zone text in the upper-right corner of iCal's main window to open the pop-up menu shown on the left.

   Choose "Other..." to open the map sheet shown below. Select a new time zone—use the "Closest City" pop-up menu or click a map location.

3. Click OK. Once you've selected alternative time zones, they remain in the time zone pop-up menu.

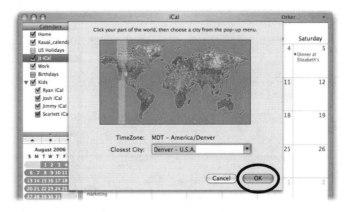

To change the time zone setting for an event:

1. Open iCal Preferences and select "Turn on time zone support" (see the previous page) to show a time zone setting in the Info drawer (circled below-left).

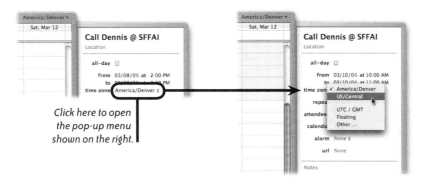

Click here to open the pop-up menu shown on the right.

2. Select an event in your calendar. Open the Info drawer—click the Show Info button, or just double-click an event to select it and open the Info drawer.

3. In the Info drawer click to the right of the **time zone** label (the text and small double-arrows), then choose one of the options in the pop-up menu (above-right).

   If you previously selected other time zones, they remain listed in the top section of this pop-up menu.

   UTC/GMT sets the time zone to Universal Time/Greenwich Mean Time—standards used as a basis for calculating time throughout most of the world.

   Choose **Floating** if you want to create events that stay at the same time, no matter what time zone you're in. For instance, a lunch event scheduled for noon will always appear in the noon time slot, no matter where you are or if you've changed the iCal time zone (as explained on the previous page) or the time zone setting in Date & Time preferences.

   Select **Other...** to show a small world map, (right). Click a time zone in the map to open a pop-up menu of cities in that time zone. Select a city, then click OK.

An event's time zone setting affects its location on the calendar. If the iCal time zone is set to San Francisco and you create a lunch event and change its time zone to Paris, the event will move nine hours back in the iCal window.

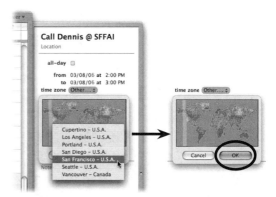

Create a To Do List

Use iCal to keep a reminder list of things you need to do.

To create a To Do list:

1. Select a calendar in the Calendars list.

   Note: When you create a To Do item, it is automatically color-coded to match the selected calendar. To switch the To Do item to a different calendar, Control-click on the To Do item, then choose another calendar from the contextual pop-up menu (shown on the left).

2. Click the To Do button in the bottom-right corner of the iCal window (the pushpin) to open the To Do pane. To resize the pane, drag the tiny dot on the left edge of the panel (circled below).

3. To create a new To Do, double-click inside the To Do pane. **Or** Control-click inside the To Do pane and select "New To Do" from the pop-up menu. **Or** from the File menu choose "New To Do."

4. To add information to a To Do item, select it in the To Do pane, then open the Info drawer. You can set a priority, set a due date, set an alarm, or switch the task to another calendar.

5. In the bottom section you can type a description, notes, comments, direction, instructions, or anything you need for the task.

After a To Do task is completed, click its checkbox in the To Do pane to mark it as completed. **Or** click its checkbox in the Info drawer (circled, below-right).

You can select **view options** for the To Do list. Click the To Do pane's title bar to open a pop-up menu and select how to sort the items (shown on the left).

The To Do list sort options.

*Choose "Hide items Outside of Calendar View" to hide To Do items that have **due dates** that are not shown in the current Calendar view.*

To Do items that don't have due dates assigned are always shown.

*You can set an alarm for a To Do item if it has a **due date** set.*

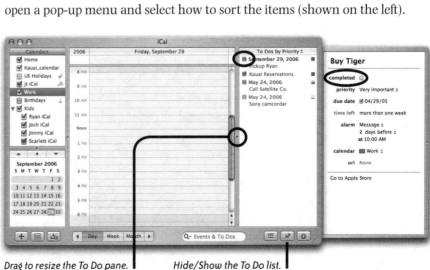

Drag to resize the To Do pane.   Hide/Show the To Do list.

Rate the priority of To Do items

You can **assign priorities** to To Do items

A **Very important** item is marked with a small icon of three horizontal bars; an **Important** item has two horizontal bars; a **Not important** item has one horizontal bar. Multiple items with the same priority are listed alphabetically within that priority group.

1. Click a To Do item to select it.

2. Click the Show Info button to open the Info drawer (shown on the right).

3. From the "priority" pop-up menu, choose a priority.

   Or you can click directly on a Priority icon (the horizontal bars in the To Do pane) to open a pop-up menu of Priority options.

A To Do item's priority is indicated by the number of horizontal bars in the icon next to it.

Click directly on the icon to change the number of bars and the priority rating.

If all three bars are dimmed, a priority has not been assigned.

The To Do Info drawer

The To Do Info drawer also has several other uses. You can:

- ▼ **Edit** a task's description.

- ▼ Check the **completed** box when a To Do task is completed. You can also do this in the To Do items pane by checking the box next to a task in the list.

- ▼ Set a **due date** that will appear above the task in the To Do pane. Setting a due date lets you set an alarm reminder.

- ▼ Switch a selected To Do item to a different calendar—from the **calendar** pop-up menu, choose a different calendar.

- ▼ Assign a **URL** (a web site address) if the task relates to information on a certain web site to which you need easy access.

- ▼ In the **Notes** area, type any additional information you need.

Hide or show various To Do lists

To Do items from different calendars all share the same To Do list. They are color-coded to match the calendar to which they belong. When you hide a calendar (uncheck its box in the Calendars list), all of the To Do items associated with that calendar are also hidden. If you have a lot of items in your To Do list, hiding some of them can make easier to find things. Or you can use the powerful search feature described on the following pages.

iCal Search

Use iCal's **search** feature to locate any event in any calendar.

To search for an event:

1. In the text entry field at the bottom of the calendar, type a keyword or phrase. All possible matches to your text entry will appear in the Search Results pane. The list of possible matches is narrowed as you continue to type.

2. When you finish typing, click the item you want. iCal shows the selected item in the main calendar area.

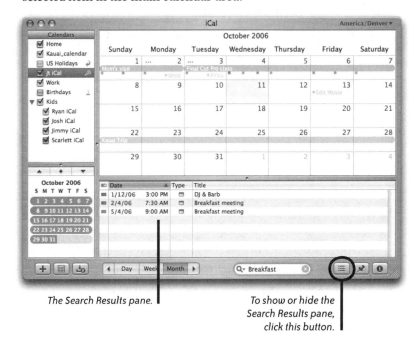

The Search Results pane.

To show or hide the Search Results pane, click this button.

To open the Info drawer for a found item, double-click the item in the Search Results pane. **Or** double-click the title bar of the found event in the calendar grid of the main View pane.

To change the information for an event, double-click the text in the event item, then type your changes. **Or** click an event to select it, then click the Show Info button to open the Info drawer. Make changes to the text in the drawer, then press Return.

Search by category

Narrow your search by choosing a specific category. Click the small triangle (shown to the right) next to the magnifying glass in the Search field to open a pop-up menu of options (shown below). Select the category you want to use, then type a keyword in the Search field.

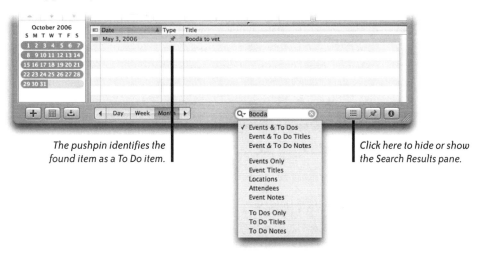

The pushpin identifies the found item as a To Do item.

Click here to hide or show the Search Results pane.

The example below shows a search for "Booda" to find her vet appointment. iCal found the information as a To Do item, indicated by the pushpin in the "Type" column of the Search Results pane. A double-click on the search result opens the Info drawer and shows all available information.

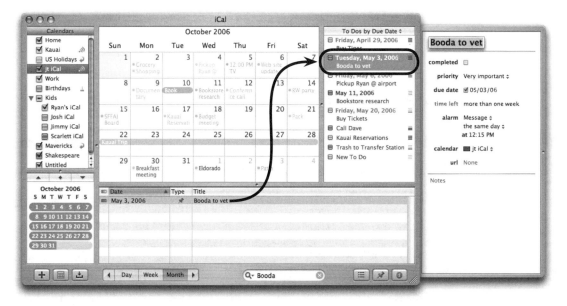

Publish an iCal Calendar

*A **broadcast** symbol in the Calendars list indicates a published calendar.*

If you want to **make your calendar available to others on the Internet,** you can publish it. Your family and/or co-workers can view your published calendar from any computer in the world using a web browser.

To publish your calendar:

1. Select a calendar in the Calendars list that you want to publish.

2. From the Calendar menu in the top menu bar, choose "Publish...." A sheet slides down into view (shown below).

To publish a calendar, of course, you must be connected to the Internet.

3. Type a name for your published calendar and check the boxes to publish changes automatically and to choose which calendar items to publish. Select an option from the "Publish on" pop-up menu:

   ▼ If you have a .Mac account, choose ".Mac" to publish your calendar to the Apple server.

   ▼ If you plan to publish to a WebDAV server (see the next page), choose "a Private Server."

4. Click the "Publish" button.

5. When your calendar has uploaded to the server, the "Calendar Published" window opens to show the address where you or others can go to view or subscribe to that particular calendar.

   To see your calendar online, click "Visit Page" (below-left).

   To notify others that you've published a calendar, click "Send Mail."

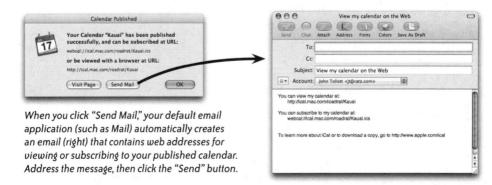

When you click "Send Mail," your default email application (such as Mail) automatically creates an email (right) that contains web addresses for viewing or subscribing to your published calendar. Address the message, then click the "Send" button.

Publish to a private server

For an alternative to publishing your calendars on the .Mac site, check iCal Exchange at www.iCalx.com. iCal Exchange offers free iCalendar publishing to its own WebDAV server.

WebDAV (Web Distributed Authoring and Versioning) servers can share calendars created using the industry-standard .ics format.

To add password protection to a published calendar, you need to publish to a Webdav server that supports password protection. Choose "Publish on: a Private Server" in iCal's Publish Calendar sheet. This option displays text fields for entering a Webdav server address and for setting a login name and password. Checkmark the options you want to use, such as "Publish changes automatically" and "Publish titles and notes."

Make changes to a published calendar

There are several ways to update your published calendar.

- ▼ **Either** select a calendar from the Calendars list, then from the Calendar menu choose "Refresh."

- ▼ **Or** select a calendar from the Calendars list, then from the Calendar menu choose "Publish." Give the calendar the exact name as the existing published one. This new, updated calendar will replace the old one.

- ▼ **Or** select a calendar from the Calendars list, then click the Show Info button. Click next to the "auto-publish" field in the Info drawer and select "after each change" from the pop-up menu (shown right).

- ▼ **Or** when you first publish a calendar, set iCal to automatically update changes: From the Calendar menu at the top of your screen, choose "Publish," then select "Publish changes automatically" in the Publish Calendar sheet (see the top of the previous page). If you have a full-time Internet connection, iCal **automatically** uploads the changes. (If you don't have a full-time connection, don't choose this option; instead, dial up and publish changes when necessary.)

Unpublish an iCal calendar

If you decide **to unpublish a published calendar,** it's easy to do: Make sure you're connected to the Internet. Select a published calendar in the Calendars list, then from the Calendar menu choose "Unpublish."

You still have the original copy of the calendar on your computer, but it's no longer available for viewing by others.

Subscribe to iCal Calendars

*A **Subscribe** symbol in the Calendars list indicates a calendar to which you've subscribed.*

You can **subscribe to calendars** that have been published by family, friends, colleagues, or total strangers. You do not have to have a .Mac account to subscribe to a calendar that's hosted on .Mac or other WebDAV servers.

To subscribe to any iCal calendar:

1. From the Calendar menu at the top of your screen, choose "Subscribe...."

2. **Either** enter the calendar URL (web address) that was given to you or that you may have received in an email from the publisher of the calendar, then click "Subscribe."

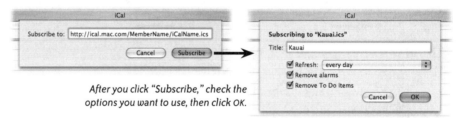

After you click "Subscribe," check the options you want to use, then click OK.

Or if you know the web address of a site that offers iCalendars for subscription (such as http://apple.com/ical/library), use your browser to visit the site and click one of the available calendar links. That address will appear immediately in the "Subscribe to" field (below-left).

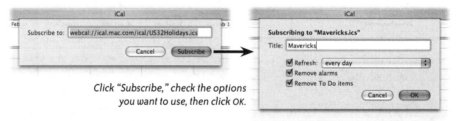

Click "Subscribe," check the options you want to use, then click OK.

3. If subscription to the calendar requires a password, an "Authentication" window opens. Enter the required user name and password, then click OK to continue.

4. The subscribed calendar appears in your Calendars list. Check its box to show it in the main viewing area.

Other calendars available for subscription

In addition to subscribing to the calendars of friends, family, and colleagues, there are many special-interest calendars available online to which you can subscribe. It's quite amazing—there are public calendars that list special events, sports teams, school calendars, religious events, movies, television, and many more. Visit these sites to see some of the possibilities:

www.apple.com/ical/library

www.iCalshare.com

www.iCalx.com

Refresh calendars

If you didn't choose the "Refresh" option when you first subscribed to a calendar (as explained on the opposite page), you can manually refresh it at any time **to see the most current version.** When you refresh , iCal downloads the current calendar from the server, ensuring that you have the latest published information.

1. Select a subscribed calendar in the Calendars list.

2. From the Calendar menu at the top of your screen, choose "Refresh."

If you don't have a full-time connection, make sure you dial up to connect to the Internet before you choose to refresh.

Backup iCal Calendars

If iCal contains valuable information, be sure to backup your calendars.

To manually backup:

1. Go to your Home folder, open the Library folder, then locate the Calendars folder. Your iCal calendars are saved here as .ics files.

2. To make a backup copy, drag the Calendars folder to another drive, or burn it to a CD or DVD.

Backup application. If you have a .Mac membership (see Chapter 4), another way to backup calendars is to use Backup. You can make backup copies of files to a local disk or to your .Mac iDisk. Download Backup from the .Mac web site if you don't already have it on your computer.

1. Open Backup. Select "Personal Data & Settings" in the Backup window. (below-left) to create a Backup Plan.

2. Click the Action button (the gear icon), then choose "Edit" to open the "Personal Data & Settings" window (below-right).

3. Create a Destination and Schedule item. Click the plus **(+)** button. In the sheet that drops down, specify a destination and schedule.

4. Click "Back Up Now." Your Backup Plan now appears in the Backup window. For future backups, select the plan, then click "Back Up."

Click "Restore..." to recover backed up files.   *Click the plus sign to add items to the Backup Plan.*

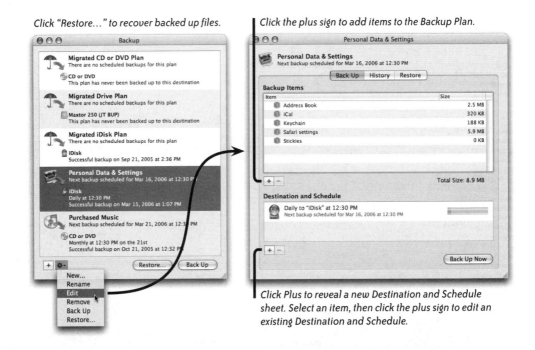

Click Plus to reveal a new Destination and Schedule sheet. Select an item, then click the plus sign to edit an existing Destination and Schedule.

Energy Saver and Fax
Tidbits for Traveling

Your Mac laptop provides *Energy Saver* settings that let you optimize your computer's performance for *battery* operation when you're on the road, or for *power adapter* operation when you're plugged in to a wall outlet and not concerned about conserving battery power.

This chapter also shows how you to send or receive faxes with your laptop. Any document that can be printed can also be faxed, if you have access to a phone line that you can plug into the laptop's modem port.

Important Energy Saver Settings

You can customize your Energy Saver settings so your laptop's power management is optimized for *battery power,* which lets you get as much computing time as possible out of your limited power supply. When you're on the go, these settings can make a difference in whether or not you run out of power before you get a chance to plug in or recharge.

To customize your Energy Saver settings, open System Preferences (from the Apple menu), then click the "Energy Saver" icon to open the window shown below.

The Options pane

Click the "Options" tab to show settings that affect power consumption and performance.

To optimize your laptop for maximum battery life:

▼ **"Settings for" pop-up menu.** Choose "Battery."

▼ **"Optimization" pop-up menu.** Choose "Better Battery Life."

To set Energy Saver settings for times when your laptop is connected to a power outlet, from this menu choose "Power Adapter" instead of "Battery."

Select "Show battery status in the menu bar" to monitor your battery power with just a glance. See the example on the following page.

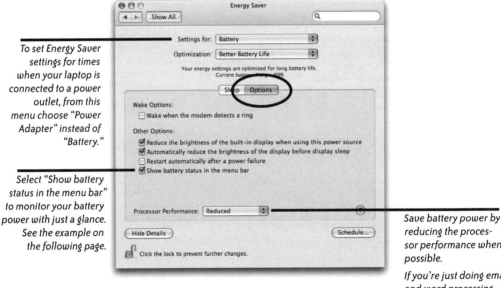

Save battery power by reducing the processor performance when possible.

If you're just doing email and word processing, you can get away with "Reduced."

If you're editing high-resolution images, you'll need "Highest."

When *Battery* is selected in "Settings for," the "Optimization" menu contains presets that optimize energy settings as *Better Battery Life, Normal, Better Performance,* or *Custom.*

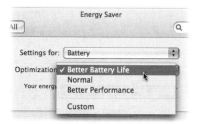

When you move the sliders (shown on the next page) to change any of the default Sleep settings, the "Optimization" pop-up menu automatically changes to "Custom."

▼ **"Show battery status in the menu bar" checkbox.** When this option is selected, the battery icon (shown below) appears in your menu bar. Click the icon to open a menu of useful Energy Saver commands.

Hover your pointer over the "Show" option to see a sub-menu from which you can choose how to display the battery status.

You can also choose to "Open Energy Saver…" from the bottom of the menu for quick and easy access to these settings.

The Sleep pane

Click the "Sleep" tab (circled below) to show settings that can lengthen the life of your battery and of your screen. Sleep is a low-power mode that conserves the battery power.

▼ **Inactivity sliders.**

Use the *top slider* to set how long the **computer** will be inactive before it puts the **hard drive** to sleep.

Use the *bottom slider* to determine how long before the display (the screen) goes to sleep. Setting the display to go to sleep after a short period of inactivity not only saves a lot of battery power, but it prolongs the life of the screen.

▼ **Put the hard disk(s) to sleep when possible.** Check the box at the bottom-left of the window to make the hard disk spin down whenever it feels a need to. For instance, while working on a project, the hard drive can go to sleep until you decide to save the file. It takes a couple of seconds to spin back up when you wake the computer (by moving the mouse, tapping a key, or saving a file). This can be inconvenient, but it's not as inconvenient as having your battery fail.

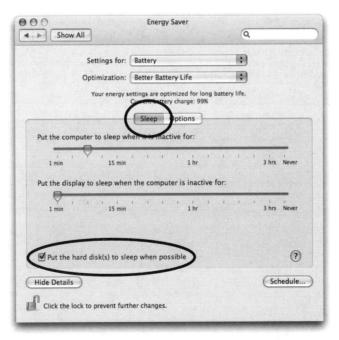

Set a schedule

Your Mac laptop lets you set a time to automatically start up or shut down your laptop. Use the pop-up menus to tell your laptop when to start up, wake up, shut down, or sleep. If you keep a pretty regular schedule, you can have your Mac wake up every morning at, say 6 A.M., so by the time you're up and showered and have had your coffee, your Mac is waiting for you. And you can be assured your Mac will shut down for you at night no matter how late you're out.

Of course, the laptop screen must be open (not necessarily awake) for the schedule to take effect appropriately.

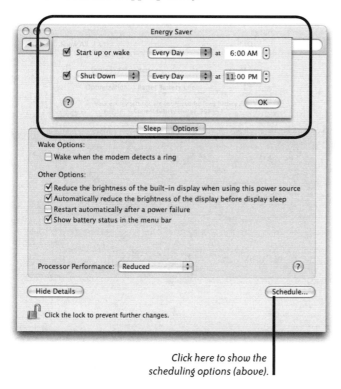

Click here to show the
scheduling options (above).

Maximize your Battery Life

In addition to the Energy Saver settings on the previous pages, there are several other steps that help maximize the life of your battery.

▼ **Keyboard illumination.** If your laptop provides it, turn off keyboard illumination: Open System Preferences, choose "Keyboard & Mouse," then click the "Keyboard" tab. Uncheck "Illuminate keyboard in low light conditions."

Or tap the F8 key on your keyboard.

▼ **Bluetooth.** Turn off Bluetooth when it's not being used:

If you've set Bluetooth status to show in the menu bar, click the Bluetooth icon and choose "Turn Bluetooth Off."

Or open System Preferences, choose "Bluetooth," then click the "Settings" tab. If Bluetooth is on, click the button to "Turn Bluetooth Off."

▼ **Dim the screen.** Dim the brightness of your screen:

Tap the F1 key on your keyboard.

Or open System Preferences, choose "Displays," then use the "Brightness" slider to dim the screen.

Drag the slider to the left to dim the screen.

Fax on the Go

Occasionally you may need to send a document to someone as a fax or you might need hard copy of a file, say for handouts at a meeting. This aging fax technology may not quite measure up to the advantages of emailing a PDF, but it works, and no one has troubling opening a fax. And darn it, some people just want a fax.

Another fax option is to sign up for an online fax service such as eFax.com. See page 210.

Faxing has occasionally come in handy in our travels when a printer wasn't available—we faxed to the hotel business office from the Mac.

Any document that you can print from your computer can also be faxed from your computer, but you must use a dial-up modem connection to send a fax. The MacBook Pro laptops do not have built-in internal modems, so if you plan to send or receive faxes, you must buy an external modem (Apple sells a USB modem in their online store).

Connect a phone line to the laptop's modem port.

To send a fax

1. Open a document that you want to fax.

2. From the File menu, choose "Print..." **or** press Command P.
   The Print sheet drops down from the document's title bar (below).

3. Click the "PDF" button, then choose "Fax PDF..." (also below).

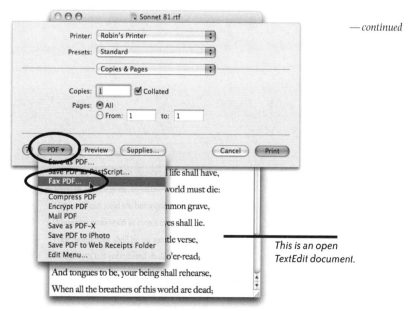

—continued

This is an open TextEdit document.

4. Enter a fax number in the "To" field (below).

   Or click the Address Book button to the right of the "To" field, then choose a fax contact from your Address Book.

5. Click the "Fax" button. If the modem is busy (with an Internet connection, for example), the fax is sent as soon as the modem is available.

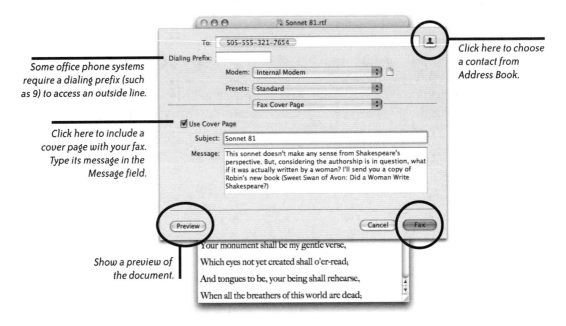

Some office phone systems require a dialing prefix (such as 9) to access an outside line.

Click here to choose a contact from Address Book.

Click here to include a cover page with your fax. Type its message in the Message field.

Show a preview of the document.

To schedule a fax:

If a phone line isn't available at the moment, you can *schedule* a fax to begin at a certain time.

1. Open a document that you want to fax.

2. Press Command P to open the Print dialog sheet (opposite page).

3. From the unnamed pop-up menu (it usually displays "Copies & Pages in the menu), choose "Scheduler."

The "Copies & Pages" pop-up menu.

4. Click the "At" button and specify a time to send the fax.

Or choose "On Hold" so you can fax the document at a future, undetermined time.

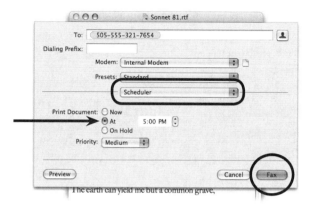

5. Click the "Fax" button to show the Fax dialog sheet (opposite page).

6. Enter the information, then click "Fax."

To check the status of a fax:

1. Click the modem icon (shown below) that appears in the Dock while you're faxing.

This modem icon appears in the Dock when a fax is sent or scheduled. Click it to open the status window shown on the next page.

2. In the modem status window (shown on the following page), check the Status column to see if the document is faxing, on hold, or stopped.

   ▾ **To resume a fax** that's on hold, select the fax in the list, then click "Resume" in the toolbar.

   ▾ **To stop all faxes,** click "Stop Jobs" in the window toolbar.
      Don't forget to click the button to "Start Jobs" before your next print or fax job!

   ▾ **To delete a fax,** select it in the list, then click "Delete" in the toolbar.

To receive a fax on your laptop:

The person sending you a fax must dial the number of the phone line that's connected to your laptop.

1. Connect a phone line to your laptop's modem port.

   If your modem is online, you cannot send or receive a fax until you disconnect from the Internet.

2. Set the Energy Saver preferences (page 138) so your laptop will not go to sleep because if it goes to sleep, it cannot receive a fax. Slide the sleep tab all the way to the right, to "Never."

3. Open System Preferences, then choose "Print & Fax."

4. Click the "Faxing" tab.

5. Click "Receive faxes on this computer."

The modem status window.

Mobility Tips
Domestic and Foreign

Whether your travels are foreign or domestic, getting connected while on the go just keeps getting easier. The number of wireless hot-spots in coffee shops, cafes, and other business locations keeps increasing, and most hotels and motels offer either an Ethernet connection, a wireless network, or a business office with Internet access. Even if you can't find a good, fast connection, you can always find a phone jack and connect to the Internet using your modem.

If you stay with friends or relatives when you travel, you can usually connect into whatever Internet connection they might use: If they have a wireless network set up, your Mac will automatically detect it. If they have a cable modem, connect to it using an Ethernet cable. Or, even better, connect the cable modem to an AirPort Express (to the right) so you can connect wirelessly.

If your friends have a dial-up modem, use an RJ-11 cable to connect your Mac to their phone jack, then enter their ISP information (or yours) into Internet Connect. You can even plug in an AirPort Express to a phone jack and use a dial-up connection wirelessly.

The widespread availability of both wired and wireless Internet connections means you no longer have to avoid visiting certain friends and relatives just because they don't have Internet access.

This chapter offers tips on how to protect your laptop and the data on it when you travel, plus dial-up connection tips, information on international roaming, and more.

An AirPort Express device can extend an existing wireless network, or it can act as a Base Station to create a wireless network. See Chapter 9 for details.

Protect Your Laptop

Be aware of thieves

Traveling with a laptop is risky business. Since state-of-the-art digital equipment is in great demand, laptops (and digital cameras) can disappear faster than you would believe—just take your eyes off your computer bag for a split second in an airport or Internet cafe and it could be gone. Be extra careful in big, busy Internet cafes in big cities. Professional thieves know that tourists usually put their bags down on the floor while they send email back home.

▾ Use a plain bag or backpack that doesn't call attention to itself as a super cool package that probably contains really expensive digital toys. A specially designed computer case is nice, but it's also a big red flag for professional thieves who would like to score big and go home early.

▾ When you're relaxing in an airport or restaurant, always keep your computer bag strap wrapped around an arm or leg. Professional thieves hang out at places like this just waiting for you to be distracted.

▾ When you visit an Internet cafe, never set your bag down next to your chair while you excitedly compose an email to your pals back home. By the time you type "Hi everyone, we're at a really cool Internet Cafe in London," your bag of digital hardware might be across the street and on its way to a lucky new owner. As Robin can tell you from personal experience, when you go to the nearest police station to report the theft, an un-surprised officr will say something like, "We get a dozen complaints a day from that cafe, miss."

▾ When going through security at an airport, keep an eye on your bag as it passes through the metal detector and comes off the conveyor belt. A theft can occur if a thief is several people ahead of you in line with an accomplice who's just in front of you and holds up the line by setting off the metal detector.

▾ Always take your computer on an airplane as a carry-on item. Checked luggage is more likely to get tossed around, banged up, lost, or stolen.

▾ Keep a copy of your computer make, model, and serial number in case you need to file a police report.

▾ Put an identification label on your computer bag or on the computer. Sometimes laptops are just misplaced instead of stolen.

Theft alarms

One way to help protect your laptop is to use a wireless proximity alarm. These alarms usually consist of two pieces, a small transmitter that you put in your computer bag and a small receiver that you keep in your pocket or on a keychain. When the two devices are separated by more than the preset distance (around 15 feet), a loud alarm goes off. Other alarm types detect any motion of the computer and cause your keychain device to make a chirping sound. You can remotely set off the alarm if your laptop is being stolen.

This is the wireless alarm I've used, from Fellowes.

To find wireless laptop alarms, search the web for "laptop theft alarms" or "laptop security systems" to find a variety of devices.

Track down a stolen laptop

As another safeguard, you can buy and install tracking software that includes a tracking service. If your laptop gets stolen, the happy new owner will probably use it to connect to the Internet. Any time your laptop connects to a phone line or the Internet, a distress signal is sent to the tracking service. This information provides the information necessary to locate the phone number and/or IP address being used by your missing computer. The tracking service works with local authorities, ISPs, and telephone companies to locate the computer. Some services even provide the ability to delete sensitive files remotely from the missing laptop.

What if a nice person finds your laptop and wants to return it? Make sure you have an identification label on the computer or computer bag with a local phone number or cell phone (not your home address), and hope that someone honest will call. Good luck.

A good place to start your search for laptop tracking services is StealthSignal's XTool Computer Tracker (**www.StealthSignal.com**). To find other options, search the web for "laptop tracking software."

Disable automatic login

Do you enter a password when you open your laptop and start up? If you're traveling with that laptop, you should. Your Mac doesn't ask for a password when you've got "automatic login" turned on. And if there's no password, then anyone who steals your Mac has access to everything on it.

As the Administrator of the laptop, you can turn off automatic login for all users, whether or not you know their passwords. See page 151.

To turn off the automatic login for your account:

1. Open System Preferences and click on "Accounts."
2. Click on your account name in the left-hand pane.
3. Click the locked icon at the bottom-left. Enter your password.
4. Click "Login Options" at the bottom of the Accounts pane.
5. Uncheck the box to "Automatically log in as."
6. Click the lock icon again to lock it up.

Secure Empty Trash

Normally, when you put files in the Trash and then "Empty Trash," the files aren't really thrown away. The file name is removed from the disk directory, but the file is still there until the computer overwrites that space on the hard disk with new data. That's why some disk utilities are able to recover files you've thrown away.

If you've moved sensitive files to the Trash, you can make sure they can't be recovered. From the Finder menu, choose "Secure Empty Trash." This command overwrites files that are in the Trash with erroneous data, making them completely unrecoverable.

Private Browsing

When you visit web sites, Safari keeps a history of where you've been so you can easily retrace your steps back to a site of interest. It also creates the possibility that curious snoopers could check to see which sites you've visited, hoping to learn something confidential about you.

But in Safari you can turn on "Private Browsing." When you do this, web pages are not added to the History menu, form information isn't saved for AutoFill (including names and passwords), search terms are not added to the pop-up menu in the the web search box, and items are automatically removed from the Downloads window. The Back and Forward buttons still work until you close the Safari window.

To turn on "Private Browsing," go to the Safari menu and choose "Private Browsing" (shown to the left). It turns itself off every time you quit, so when you restart Safari, you'll have to turn it back on again.

To turn off private browsing, return to the Safari menu and choose "Private Browsing" again to remove the checkmark next to it. Or quit Safari.

Empty the cache

You might also want to choose "Empty Cache..." from the Safari menu whenever you're finished working on the Internet so no one can go see which pages you've been to recently by looking in your cache folder.

Clear the History

At any time, whether or not you are using "Private Browsing," you can always go to the History menu and choose "Clear History" to get rid of the list of web pages you've visited.

Extra security features

The Security preferences offer several security features that won't prevent your laptop from getting stolen, but will prevent thieves from having access to your data.

Open System Preferences and choose "Security."

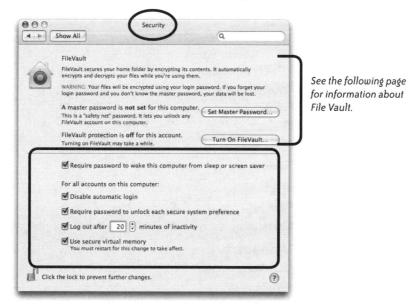

See the following page for information about File Vault.

▼ **Require password to wake this computer from sleep or screen saver.**
If you have your laptop set to sleep after a certain number of minutes or if you have a screen saver set to go on, this feature helps to safeguard your files when you leave the computer unattended—if it has gone to sleep or the screen saver has turned on, someone must enter the password to get back to the screen. *This is incredibly useful if your laptop gets stolen while it's already turned on*—as soon as someone shuts the lid and puts it to sleep, they won't be able to get back in. Ha.

▼ **Disable automatic login.** Now anyone using your computer must enter the correct login password.

See page 149 for another way to turn off automatic login.

▼ **Log out after _ minutes of activity.** This lets you set how soon after being unattended your laptop will log out. Make sure it requires a password to log back in.

Encrypt your Home folder with FileVault

For serious privacy, **data encryption** is the solution. Encryption scrambles the selected data and it can only be unscrambled by entering the correct password.

For total data security, use FileVault. FileVault encrypts your entire Home folder using 128-bit AES encryption (theoretically un-hackable). It protects the entire contents of your Home folder, yet you can work with your files.

This might be most important in this kind of scenario: You're working on your laptop, get distracted, and someone swipes it right out from under you. You've got your sleep feature password-protected (see the previous page), so he can't get to your data. So the disgusting little creep who stole your laptop slithers home, inserts a startup disk, and proceeds to reinstall the operating system, but doesn't replace your Home folder and files, hoping to get to them. Aha! Foiled again—if you've got FileVault turned on.

1. Open System Preferences and choose "Security."
2. Click "Set Master Password" and set a password and a hint.
3. Click "Turn on FileVault..." to start FileVault. This can take well over an hour, depending on how much and what you have on your laptop.

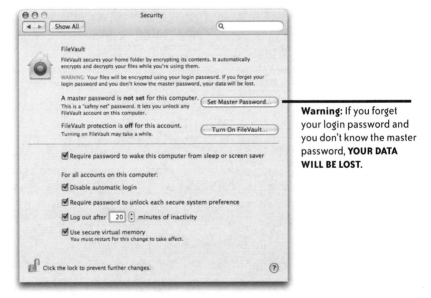

The master password also lets you, as Administrator, change the password for any other account on the laptop, in case another user forgot hers.

Warning: If you forget your login password and you don't know the master password, **YOUR DATA WILL BE LOST.**

Once turned on and enabled with a master password, FileVault automatically encrypts and decrypts data on the fly.

Encrypt only selected files and folders

If you have just a few files or folders you want to make secure, you may not want to use FileVault to encrypt your *entire* Home folder. Instead, you can store critical data inside an encrypted, password-protected *disk image*. This is not an "on-the-fly" feature; that is, you will have to open the disk image every time you want to use the file.

To make a disk image:

1. Put all the files you want to encrypt into a single folder. (Always be sure you've got backup disks of important files somewhere else!)
2. Open Disk Utility (it's in the Utilities folder, inside the Applications folder). The window (below) shows your hard disk in the left column. Any external disks that are connected will also appear in this list.
3. Select the volume (disk) that contains the folder you want to encrypt.

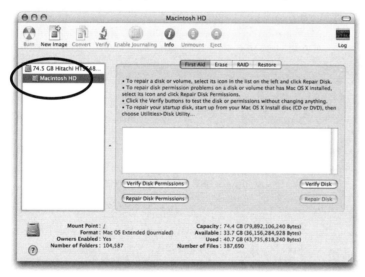

A disk image is a package of data, useful for storing files or for transferring files to others. You can choose to encrypt, compress, and/or password-protect the data.

Projects1.dmg

A disk image looks like this. Double-click it when you want to open it. You'll get an icon that looks like a removable drive, as shown below.

Projects1

Double-click this white drive icon. Your files are inside. If you chose the "read/write" format (see the next page), you can open and make changes to these files, add more files to the window, and they are all still encrypted.

Once you open a disk image, it is available **without a password** until you log out and back in again.

(In the Desktop window, this icon looks like a folder, not a drive.)

4. From the File menu, choose "New," then choose "Disk Image from Folder...," as shown below.

—continued

5. In the "Select Folder to Image" window (shown below), select the folder that you want to turn into a disk image. Click the "Image" button.

6. In the "New Image From Folder" window (below-left), name the disk image and choose a location to save it to.

From the "Image Format" pop-up menu, choose:

- ▼ **read/write** if you want to add other files later and make changes to files.

- ▼ **read only** if you *don't* need to add or change the files.

- ▼ **compressed** if you don't need to add files later *and* if you want to save as much disk space as possible

- ▼ **DVD/CD master** if you want to make exact copies of a disk. This is the format you choose to create a bootable disc.

From the "Encryption" pop-up menu, chose "AES-128."

Warning: If you forget this password, **YOUR DATA WILL BE LOST.**

7. Click "Save." An "Authenticate" alert box opens (below-right). Enter a password; do NOT check "Remember password." Click OK.

*For the best security, **DO NOT** check the box to "Remember password (add to Keychain)." If you add the password to Keychain, the disk image can be opened without typing the password.*

Secure your Sharing preferences

When connected to a network (wireless or wired), you can prevent access to folders on your computer. Use the "Sharing" preferences.

1. Open System Preferences and choose "Sharing." In the "Sharing" window, click the "Services" tab.

2. In the list, *turn off* services that are turned on (check a box to remove its checkmark). **Or** click on a service to select it, then click the "Stop" button.

3. Click the "Firewall" tab (below-right) to show the Firewall pane.

4. Click the "Start" button to turn the Firewall on. The firewall allows incoming communication to any services in the list that you checked in the Services pane. All other inbound network connections are denied.

If you need to access another computer on the network, make sure you both have "Personal File Sharing" turned on.

Firewall status message (On or Off).

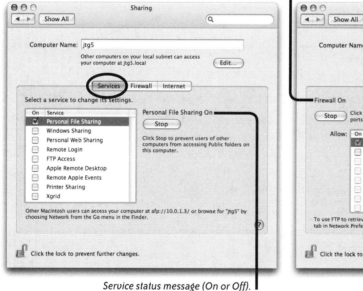

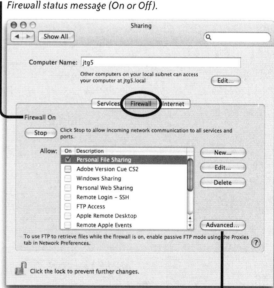

Service status message (On or Off).

Advanced firewall settings.

Advanced firewall settings

Make your computer even more secure with advanced firewall settings: Click the "Advanced" button (above-right), then checkmark "Block UDP Traffic" (used by some servers that may interfere with some network applications, such as Voice over IP), "Enable Firewall Logging" (creates a firewall activity log), and "Enable Stealth Mode" (ensures that uninvited network traffic receives no response—and makes hacking your computer nearly impossible).

SMTP Away from Home

SMTP (Simple Mail Transfer Protocol): the standard by which email is delivered on the Internet.

When you're away from the usual Internet connection at your home or office, your existing SMTP setting in Mail probably won't work and you won't be able to send outgoing email.

When you use your home/office connection, the SMTP server at your ISP recognizes you and sends your messages. But when you take your laptop to a different network or connection, your SMTP server isn't recognized and your computer can't send messages out. Instead, a sheet drops down from the title bar of your message, as shown below.

One solution is to use web-based email, such as .Mac Mail (see Chapter 4). This works just fine, but we prefer the convenience of sending email straight from our email client (Mail), just as if we were at home. Plus, you may own a domain name that you prefer to have appear in the return address of your message (*jt@ratz.com*, for instance), instead of a provider's name (such as *myname@gmail.com*)

To do this, you can subscribe to an inexpensive SMTP service that *relays* your outgoing email though their servers. Search the web for "SMTP services," or check out **SMTP.com** or **AuthSMTP.com.**

When you sign up with an SMTP service, you'll register *your email address* with the service. Enter the SMTP service provider's information into your Server Settings (shown on the following page). When you're on the go, you can choose this SMTP setting to send mail out *from the email address you registered with.*

Choose an SMTP plan that meets your mobility needs. A wide range of plans are available that offer choices in duration (one month to several years) and the number of email relays allowed per day or per month. If you're a casual Road Warrior who just wants to keep in touch, the smallest, most affordable plan should be adequate.

SMTP Server Settings

After you sign up for SMTP service and register an email address with them, all you have to do is enter that service's SMTP information in your Server Settings. The steps below are based on an SMTP.com account. The setup procedure for other providers is similar.

1. Open Mail Preferences (from the Mail menu, choose "Preferences…").

2. Click the "Accounts" button in the toolbar.

3. From the Accounts list on the left side of the window, select the email account you want to use while on the go.

4. Click the "Account Information" tab, if it isn't already.

5. From the "Outgoing Mail Server" pop-up menu, choose "Add Server…." You'll see the drop-down sheet shown below.

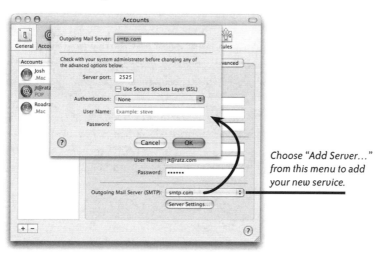

Choose "Add Server…" from this menu to add your new service.

6. In the "Outgoing Mail Server" field, type "smtp.com" (or whatever address your chosen service says to use).

7. In the "Server port" field, type "2525" (or whatever port number your chosen service says to use).

8. Follow the instructions from your SMTP provider (if any) for the other settings. (No other settings were required for our setup.)

9. Click OK. When you close the preferences, you'll be asked to save the setting.

SMTP.com (or the address of whatever service you chose) is now added to the "Outgoing Mail Server" menu in the "Accounts Information" window (shown above and also on the following page).

SMTP.com:
A *one-month* account that allows up to 50 email relays per day costs $9.99.

AuthSMTP.com:
A *one-year* account that allows up to 1000 email relays per month costs $24.

Visit the providers' web sites for detailed and current information.

Now, when you're on the go, before you send a message, choose "smtp.com" (or whatever your service's address is) from the "Outgoing Mail Server" pop-up menu (shown below).

Remember, the SMTP account is registered to a specific email address.

The SMTP address for each service is listed in this menu.

If you forget to change the Outgoing Mail Server address, the sheet shown below appears and tells you Mail cannot send the message. However, now that you've added the SMTP address, you can choose it from the sheet's pop-up menu, as shown below (if you're using the email account you registered). After you select "smtp.com" (or whatever your service's address happens to be), click "Use Selected Server." Your message is sent right away and you get to enjoy that Road Warrior thing.

Select the SMTP service's address that you added.

Dial-up Tips

If you travel to small towns or remote areas and getting connected is critical, you may not want to trust that you'll find an Internet cafe or a hotel with broadband Internet access. In this case, an old-fashioned dial-up account can be useful. No matter how small a town is, the local hotels and motels usually have telephones, allowing you to connect to the Internet by using your laptop's modem to dial an ISP number.

Local access phone numbers and 800 numbers

If you have a dial-up account, check to see if your ISP's web site offers local access numbers in the area you'll be traveling. Many ISPs do, and some also provide 800 numbers that can be used in areas where they don't provide local access numbers.

Of course, if you're desperate, you can always set up Internet Connect to dial your local ISP number long-distance (just add "1" and the ISP's area code to the "Telephone Number" field; see Chapter 3, pages 35 and 45), but that can be very expensive if you need to be online for more than a few minutes.

An 800 number from an ISP is usually on a pay-as-you-use-it basis, and the per minute fee is probably going to be more affordable than ordinary long-distance charges. Your ISP's web site should provide per-minute rate information for using 800 numbers. As of this writing, EarthLink listed its 800 service rate at $0.10/minute ($6/hour).

Does your laptop have a modem?

Most Mac laptops have modems built-in, although you may never have used yours. The newest Mac laptops, such as the MacBook Pro, do *not* include internal modems. If you have one of the new laptops, you'll need to add an external modem if you plan to connect via a dial-up connection (or if you plan to fax from your laptop). The online Apple Store web site sells a small, inexpensive modem that plugs into a Mac's USB port, shown to the right.

A USB modem.

Dial-up by the month

With the widespread availability of broadband Internet access (cable, DSL, Wi-Fi), many people no longer have dial-up accounts that they can use when on the go. If you know you'll need dial-up access while on a trip, search the web for ISPs that offer dial-up connectivity by the month. Search for "short term dial-up service" to find a provider whose terms are reasonable. Some resorts and hotels offer short-term ISP accounts with unlimited access for periods as short as one week. If getting connected in challenging situations is really critical, consider keeping a dial-up ISP account in addition to whatever broadband ISP account you may have.

NetZero, a national ISP in the U.S., offers Mac users the NetZero Platinum Plan (a monthly plan with no commitment) for just under $10/month.
www.NetZero.net

International Roaming

If you travel to another country, you'll probably be able to find Wi-Fi broadband connections that you can use. But just in case you don't, check to see if your ISP offers international roaming (sometimes called "global roaming"). Roaming services provide access to local dial-up numbers in other countries.

EarthLink.net offers subscribers international roaming for $0.15/minute.

Dialer.net is an international Internet access provider that offers dial-up, tollfree, Wi-Fi, and broadband access in more than 150 countries.

Your ISP should provide a list of international access numbers on their web site. Create a text file of the access numbers that are available for the country you'll travel to. If you can't find a Wi-Fi or broadband connection, at least you'll have the information necessary to set up Internet Connect with dial-up information.

TheList.com is a web site that provides a comprehensive list of ISPs around the world. You can also search the web for "global roaming services" or "international Internet service providers."

Configure Mail for International Roaming

International travel doesn't make it harder to *receive* email on your laptop. As long as you can connect to the Internet, Mac OS X Mail will go out and collect your email. There is, however, an issue with *sending* email when you're not directly connected to your usual ISP. You'll need to change Mail's preferences settings for "Outgoing Mail Server (SMTP)" to work with whatever service you're using while on the go. For instance, EarthLink's instructions for their International Roaming service say to change the SMTP server setting to *smtpauth.earthlink.net*.

See pages 156–158 to learn how to change your SMTP setting for Mail and about using a paid service such as **smtp.com.**

Set your modem to ignore dial tones

Modems sometimes don't recognize foreign dial tones and will fail to connect. If you have trouble connecting and suspect this is the problem, tell your modem not to wait for a dial tone.

1. Open System Preferences, then choose "Network."

2. In the Network window, from the "Show" pop-up menu, choose "Internal Modem," then click the "Modem" tab.

   If you don't see "Internal Modem" in the "Show" menu, it's because it's not turned on: Choose "Network Port Configurations" from the "Show" menu and put a check in the box for "Internal Modem." Click the "Apply Now" button at the bottom of the window. Now you'll be able to choose "Internal Modem" from the "Show" menu.

3. Click to *remove* the checkmark from the option, "Wait for dial tone before dialing."

4. Click "Apply Now."

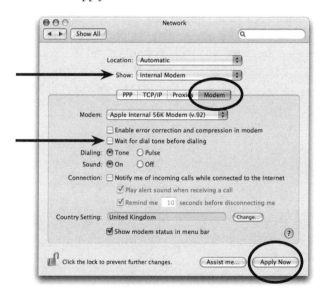

Reversed polarity, digital systems, and other risks

Whether your travel is domestic or foreign, there are a couple of other dial-up connection issues of which you should be aware.

Many hotels and office buildings use digital systems that use higher currents than your modem can handle. This type of connection can potentially damage your modem and your computer.

Another common problem is reverse polarity, a condition of incorrect wiring that can prevent a successful dial-up connection.

Buy a small, inexpensive device called a **line tester** (also known as a **modem saver**) that can test the phone line for excess current *and* reversed polarity in a phone jack. Warning lights on the device tell you if the line is safe to use, and can reverse the polarity if necessary. These devices sometimes include surge protection. Search online for "modem saver" or "line tester."

Tax impulse filters

Some countries (Austria, Belgium, Czech Republic, Germany, Slovakia, Spain, and Switzerland) use tax impulsing to monitor the length of telephone calls for billing purposes. It can cause data errors or even make you lose your dial-up connection. An inline tax impulse filter can prevent such problems. Search online for "tax impulse filter" if you think you'll need one. It's small, not much bigger than a writing pen.

Wi-Fi and Hotspots
A Wireless Primer

Wi-Fi is a specific type of wireless network that is very common. Wi-fi and hotspots are two factors that contribute most to making mobile computing convenient, useful, and fun. If your Mac laptop has an AirPort Card installed, it can detect any Wi-Fi network.

Hotspots are public Wi-Fi networks, most commonly found at Internet cafes, coffee shops, and hotels. A hotspot can be an **open** or **closed network.**

An *open network* is accessible and doesn't require a password. Sometimes it's planned that way with Internet access provided as a service. In other cases, it may be a private network that just hasn't been secured with a password. You can use any open network that your Mac laptop detects, but you may get scolded by the owner when she sees you sitting on the front steps of her office.

A *closed network* is password-protected. It might be a private network for one person, a group of friends, or an entire office. Or it might be a paid membership network that you can subscribe to by the hour, day, or month—such as the T-Mobile HotSpots found at many Starbucks coffee shops. Just order a latte and do the Road Warrior thing.

What is Wi-Fi?

Wi-Fi (Wireless Fidelity) lets you connect to the Internet wirelessly if your Mac is equipped with a wireless AirPort card *and* if you're within range of a wireless base station that's sending out a wireless Internet signal. Most wireless networks today—those found in homes, cafes, and hotels—are meant to cover small areas and are known as WLANs (Wireless Local Area Networks).

Geeky techno stuff

Wi-Fi technology is based on the IEEE (Institute of Electrical and Electronics Engineers) 802.11 family of wireless network standards created by the Wi-Fi Alliance, an independent organization that tests and certifies Wi-Fi products, and is responsible for promoting Wi-Fi technology.

The newer 802.11g standard is backwards-compatible with older 802.11b hardware.

Wi-Fi includes several versions of the 802.11 standards, with new versions being developed for the very near future. Currently the two most common are 802.11**b** (the first AirPort Base Stations and AirPort cards use this version) and 802.11**g,** which is advertised as five times faster than 802.11**b**.

When you see wireless cards or modems advertised with specific Internet speeds, keep in mind that these are always optimum **theoretical speeds.** Your **actual speed** of downloading or uploading will be substantially slower due to something called "network overhead." The diagram below shows some typical Internet connections and their advertised speeds.

Broadband speeds start around 500 kbps (kilobits per second), which is fast enough to listen to streaming music or watch streaming video. As you can see below, both versions of Wi-Fi are well within the range of broadband, even considering their actual speeds instead of their theoretical speeds.

The typical line-of-sight range for a current Wi-Fi network (b or g) is around 300 feet, depending on interference issues such as nearby buildings or thick walls (here in New Mexico, three-foot walls are not uncommon). Other versions of Wi-Fi are on the way that promise increased speed and range. See the next page for a glimpse of the Wi-Fi future.

Typical Internet connection types and speeds

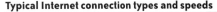
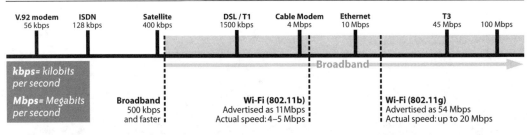

Wireless Internet technologies

There are wireless Internet technologies that exist besides Wi-Fi, and more that are being developed. One you may be able to take advantage of right now is EVDO; see Chapter 11. Below are more details about Wi-Fi and WiMAX.

▾ **802.11b** (11 Mbps) and **802.11g** (54 Mbps). Besides these two standards, there are several other versions lurking just around the corner that will enhance our mobile computing experiences. Of course, when these technologies are available, you'll need to install a compatible wireless card to take advantage of them. Wireless technology is also an example of the "format wars" we've seen in video and DVD formats. It remains to be seen which technologies will be big-time and long-term players.

▾ **802.11n.** This standard is expected to be approved in early 2007 or sooner. Described as the next generation of 802.11 standards, 802.11n uses multiple wireless antennas to transmit and receive data, and claims speeds in excess of 100 Mbps. The range is expected to be greater than existing Wi-Fi.

Products called "Pre-n" (such as wireless modems and routers) are already on the market, claiming throughput speeds that are impressive. There's no guarantee that Pre-n products will be compatible with the final 802.11n specifications.

▾ **WiMAX (802.16).** This standard is designed for wireless metropolitan area networks (MAN). While it's too technical and expensive for average home users, it's a promising solution for providing wireless access to entire neighborhoods or cities. WiMAX proponents claim a range of up to 30 miles in areas where there's an unobstructed line of sight, and 3 to 5 miles in city areas where buildings cause interference. Speeds of 75 Mbps are also claimed, but these are theoretical numbers. The latest market research predictions say WiMAX will be widely available after 2009.

Many other wireless standards being developed, but these are the ones you're most likely to hear about in the near future. Good ol' Wi-Fi (802.11 standards) will remain popular, mainly because its price tag is likely to stay far below the others.

If you want to stay informed on the latest wireless technologies and products, check some of the web sites devoted to just that—search the web for "Wi-Fi news." One good source for great wireless information, news, product reviews, and tips is the JiWire weeklywire newsletter. At **JiWire.com** you can register for a free JiWire membership that includes the email newsletter.

Where and How to Find Hotspots

When you're out and about in an unfamiliar place, there are many different ways to find a nearby hotspot. First of all, check for a local Starbucks coffee shop. They seem to be everywhere, and many of them are T-Mobile HotSpots (see below). T-Mobile also has a presence at FedEx Kinko's Office and Print Centers, selected hotels, airline clubs, and airports.

Other wireless providers such as Boingo and FreedomLink provide similar services in other locations. FreedomLink hotspots are at selected UPS Stores, McDonald's restaurants, Barnes & Noble bookstores, Mail Boxes Etc. locations, and other venues that range from airports to coffee shops. If you have an existing hotspot membership with a certain provider, you'll want to find a location that uses that provider.

Hotspots often have a window sticker near the front door that advertises Wi-Fi availability and identifies the provider. If you don't find one of these high-profile hotspot locations, try one or more of the following techniques.

Paid Wi-Fi hotspot memberships

Some venues provide Wi-Fi for free; other places use a paid membership service, such as the T-Mobile HotSpots at Starbucks all over the world. When you connect to a Wi-Fi signal at Starbucks, the login page (that you can see for free) lets you login with your membership name and password. If you don't have a membership, you can buy one online, on the spot—a day pass, pay as you go, or monthly—then surf away. Since Starbucks coffee shops are everywhere, we like to keep a T-Mobile wireless membership. If we can't find a T-Mobile HotSpot, we buy a one-day pass from any hotspot we can find.

Finding hotspots

How do you find Wi-Fi Spots? If you have a paid hotspot membership, your provider should have a list of spots on their web site. You can also visit many different sites that provide lists of hotspots: **JiWire.com, WiFinder.com, wi-here.com, Wi-FiHotspotList.com, WiFiPlanet.com,** and **WiFiFreeSpot.com.**

JiWire.com has a free Dashboard Widget (shown on the left) that lets you search for Hotspots. You can limit the search to "Paid" or "Free" hotspots, or both. Go to **JiWire.com** and enter "widget" in the home page search field. Or go to **Apple.com,** click the "Mac OS X" tab, then click the "Widgets" link. On the Widgets page, enter "JiWire" in the search field. Of course, you need to do this when you have a connection!

JiWire's Hotspot Finder Dashboard Widget.

Download an offline hotspot directory

JiWire.com provides a free software utility called "Hotspot Locator" for Mac. When you *do* have an Internet connection, the software checks the JiWire servers for updated hotspot information and updates itself. Be sure to update the JiWire Locator before you leave on a trip, and you'll have a current resource at your fingertips.

Use your laptop as a Wi-Fi detector

If you're driving around in a car and have a co-pilot to watch the laptop screen, you can turn on AirPort and let it search for a wireless network. This is called "war-driving." If the AirPort status icon in the menu starts showing a strong signal, pull over and see if you can connect to it. If it's a *closed node* (password protected), you won't be able join the network. If it's an *open node* (no password protection), you should be able to use it.

You don't really need a car. Walking is even better because it gives you more time to detect networks in an area. However, walking around holding an open laptop looks suspicious, if not downright weird. It's less conspicuous to walk around with a Wi-Fi detector (see below) or a Wi-Fi enabled PDA.

There are arguments over whether or not it's ethical or legal to use a network you find on the street. If you're desperate for a connection and don't have malicious intentions, use the network for your emergency connection. Be polite and very apologetic if the network owner approaches you and asks what you're doing.

Use a handheld Wi-Fi detector

Wi-Fi detectors are small, handheld devices that detect Wi-Fi signals. They can indicate the strength of the detected signal and, in some cases, tell you the name of the network and whether it's open or closed. Some models can even determine the direction the signal is coming from. Often we've turned on our Wi-Fi detector in a hotel room just out of curiosity and been surprised to find a wireless network right there. Or, as was the case in a hotel in Egypt, aWi-Fi network was accessible from our balcony, but nowhere else in the room.

The Canary Wireless Digital HotSpotter shows the network name, signal strength, channel, and open/closed status.

Search the Internet for "wifi finder" or "wifi seeker." Or start your search at **Kensington.com** or **CanaryWireless.com.**

Hotspot membership logins in other countries

If you have a hotspot membership, your login in another country may be slightly different than it is at home. For instance, if your T-Mobile membership login user name is *roadwarrior*, when you travel to Europe you may have to log in as *roadwarrior@t-mobile.us*. Check with your hotspot provider to see if they require login modifications like this in other countries. Or, ask for a tech support person at the foreign cafe you're in—that's how we learned this tip.

Look for war-chalking signs

Open node.

Closed node.

In certain metropolitan areas, Wi-Fi networks are everywhere—even overlapping each other. Some Wi-Fi users have started a practice of using chalk to draw symbols on sidewalks or building walls to mark the areas where they've detected a Wi-Fi network. This is called "war-chalking" and is based on the depression-era hobo practice of using symbols to mark houses as friendly, bad dog, good food, etc.

In war-chalking, the symbol for an **open node** (a wireless signal without password protection) is made of two back-to-back semicircles (top-left). The symbol for a **closed node** (a wireless network that has password protection) is a closed circle (bottom-left).

AirPort Extreme and AirPort Express

Both AirPort Extreme and AirPort Express (a miniature, portable version of AirPort Extreme) Base Stations convert wired Internet connections into wireless (Wi-Fi) networks.

Plug the AirPort Extreme into a power outlet.

Let's say you're in a **hotel room** that has a broadband Internet connection in the form of an Ethernet port near a desk (it might be labeled as a "data port"). Instead of having to do your online business at the desk, you can connect your AirPort Express to the Ethernet port and set up your own wireless network for the room, then use your laptop anywhere in the room.

Plug an Ethernet cable in here, and connect it to your broadband modem. If you're in a hotel, plug it into the room's Ethernet data port.

Or perhaps at your **home/office** you subscribe to broadband through a cable company (or other provider) and they set up a broadband modem that's connected via Ethernet cable to a desktop Mac. If the modem has an extra, unused Ethernet port, connect another Ethernet cable from the empty modem port to your AirPort Express device, then plug the AirPort Express into a power outlet (diagram below). (Of course you can also connect the broadband modem to an AirPort Extreme Base Station; see the diagram on the following page.)

Now you can connect your laptop to the Internet wirelessly from any room in your house (depending on the size of your house, and if other signal interference factors are minimal). You can realistically expect a wireless range of 100–150 feet.

If you already have an existing wireless network, use an AirPort Express to *extend* the network to areas of the house or office that don't have adequate signal strength. Just plug the AirPort Express into a power outlet in another room. AirPort Express picks up the existing Wi-Fi signal and relays it to the surrounding areas (this is also how we get iTunes from our office to the speakers in the kitchen). See the following page.

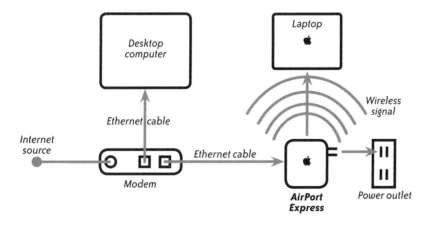

Extend the range with AirPort Express

This diagram shows how you can set up a wireless network and *extend the range* of the network by plugging an AirPort Express into a power outlet in another room. If you don't have an AirPort Extreme, you can use an AirPort Express in its place.

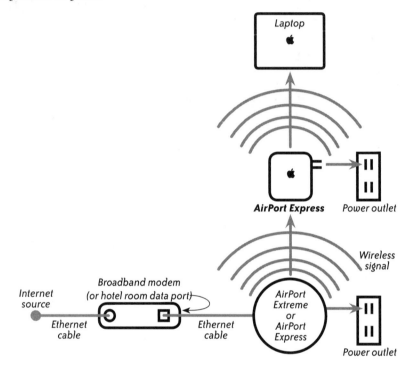

AirPort Base Stations

The older, full-sized AirPort Base Stations support only the 802.11**b** Wi-Fi standard. The newer, full-sized AirPort Base Stations support both 802.11**b** *and* 802.11**g** standards (five times faster) and are called AirPort *Extreme* Base Stations. An AirPort Extreme Base Station (below-right) provides more ports than the smaller AirPort Express (below-left).

These are the ports on an AirPort Extreme Base Station:

- ▾ **External Antenna.** You can add an external antenna to increase the range of your signal or to cover "dead spots" in the signal's coverage.

- ▾ **WAN (Wide Area Network).** Use an Ethernet cable to connect to a network or to a broadband modem.

- ▾ **LAN (Local Area Network).** Use an Ethernet cable to connect to an existing network, a computer, or an Ethernet hub.

- ▾ **RJ-11.** Use a telephone cable (RJ-11) to connect to a phone line for wireless dial-up connections.

- ▾ **USB.** Use an Ethernet cable to connect a USB printer or scanner.

- ▾ **Power.** Plug the power cord from the base station into a power outlet.

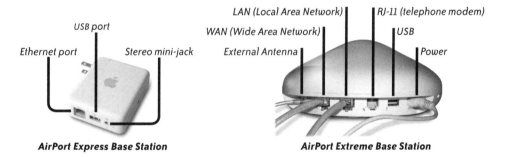

AirPort Express Base Station

AirPort Extreme Base Station

The stereo mini-jack on the AirPort Express lets you connect powered stereo speakers and stream music wirelessly from iTunes to wherever your AirPort Express and speakers are located.

Test your AirPort connection

To test your wireless connection, open Safari. When your home page opens, click a link and see if it works. If the connection doesn't seem to be working, open **AirPort Setup Assistant.** You'll find it in the Utilities folder, which is inside your Applications folder. Follow the step-by-step instructions.

This is the AirPort Admin Utility window. The name of your AirPort Extreme Base Station or your AirPort Express Base Station appear in the left column. If you use both, both names appear in the list.

To change the Base Station name, password, or security setting, double-click the name in the list. The window shown below opens.

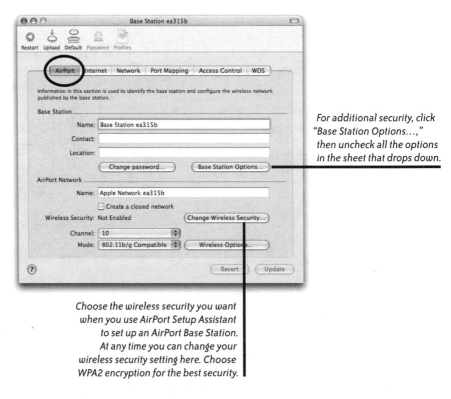

For additional security, click "Base Station Options...," then uncheck all the options in the sheet that drops down.

Choose the wireless security you want when you use AirPort Setup Assistant to set up an AirPort Base Station. At any time you can change your wireless security setting here. Choose WPA2 encryption for the best security.

Also, check the **Network settings** in System Preferences:

▼ In the "Network Port Configurations" pane, make sure "AirPort" is checkmarked. Drag "AirPort" to the top of the list if you want the wireless connection to have priority over other connection types (see pages 27–28).

▼ Put a checkmark next to "Show AirPort status in menu bar" (shown on page 32) so you can quickly check your AirPort connection and signal strength.

The number of bars in the AirPort status icon indicates the strength of your Wi-Fi signal.

You can also check the wireless signal strength in **Internet Connect.** Choose "Open Internet Connect..." from the AirPort status menu (shown above). In the Internet Connect window that opens, click the "AirPort" button. See page 40 for details.

Wi-Fi Security

When you join a Wi-Fi network, be aware of a few basic security cautions.

▼ If you've set up your own AirPort wireless network, encrypt the net-work and set a network password. AirPort Admin Utility allows you to choose WEP or WPA2 security. WEP is not very secure. WPA2 is much stronger and very secure, using the Advanced Encryption Standard (AES). Page 172 shows how to turn on AirPort security using AirPort Admin Utility.

▼ Turn off "Personal File Sharing" (in Sharing preferences) if you're not using it. You don't need it to open web pages or send and receive email (see page 155).

▼ Turn on your laptop's firewall to prevent uninvited connections (see page 155).

▼ A computer-to-computer network (also known as an *ad hoc* network) lets you share files directly with another computer with a wireless card, even when there's no Internet connection at all. You should protect this network with WEP security. WEP is not as secure as WPA2, but it's the only option when you create an ad hoc network. You can choose between 40-bit and 128-bit (128-bit is more secure, of course) encryption from the "WEP key" pop-up menu. See pages 189–190 for details about how to set up and use a computer-to-computer network.

File Sharing
On the Go

The advantages of traveling with a laptop range from having fun to getting important work done on time. And getting work done often involves being able to share files and information with other people.

Sometimes you need access to the files on a computer that's just a few feet away. Or you may need to share files with someone anywhere else in the world.

All you need is a network connecting you and the other computer. The network might be the Internet; a wireless network (such as Wi-Fi); a hard-wired, local network (such as cables connecting devices); or a combination of two or more networking techniques.

The network might even be *sneakernet,* where someone physically carries files between computers on a disc or some portable medium. That may sound primitive and low-tech, but it works.

In fact, a handy travel tip is to carry blank CDs and DVDs so you'll have them when you need them. Even if you *can* easily find blank discs to buy, they might cost many times more than you're used to paying.

This chapter covers a variety of sharing techniques for when you're on the go. And, of course, the same file sharing tips work at home, in a local coffee shop, or at the office.

Check your System Preferences

To share files over a network, make sure a network is activated and that you have enabled "Personal File Sharing," explained below.

Check the Network preferences

To activate the desired network:

1. Open System Preferences, then choose "Network."
2. In the "Network" window (below-left), choose "Network Port Configurations" from the "Show" pop-up menu.
3. Check the box next to the network you want to use. If more than one network is checked, drag the *preferred* network to the top of the list.
4. Click "Apply Now" to apply any changes you made.

Check the Sharing preferences

To turn on Personal File Sharing:

1. Open System Preferences, then choose "Sharing."
2. In the "Sharing" window (below-right), click the "Services" tab, then check "Personal File Sharing."

Show the "Network Port Configurations" pane.

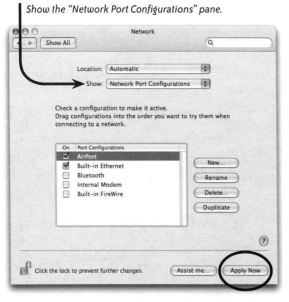

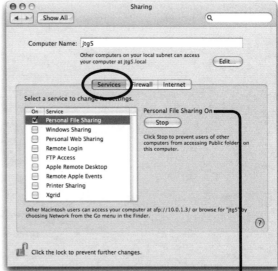

This message confirms that "Personal File Sharing" is on.

Archive Files and Folders before Sharing

When you plan to send a file (or a folder full of files) across a network, you should create a compressed copy that takes less disk space and less time to transfer. A compressed file or collection of files is called an **archive.** Making an archive also helps prevent the file from getting corrupted along the way. (Don't compress PDF files because they're already compressed.)

To create an archive:

1. Select a file or a folder full of files.

   Or select more than one file; you can compress a group of selected files into one archive.

2. From the File menu, choose "Create Archive."

   Or Control-click the item and choose "Create Archive" from the contextual pop-up menu (shown below-left).

   The finished archive will be in the same folder as the original files.

Control-click on an item, then
choose "Create Archive."

Web Receipts.zip
An archived file icon.

To open an archived file to convert it to its original, uncompressed state, double-click it.

iChat File Sharing

The easiest way to share files with another Mac user over the Internet is to use iChat, the instant messaging software that's built-in to Mac OS X. iChat works through an Internet connection. It knows when people in your Buddy List are online and shows their names in the Buddy List window (shown below).

iChat isn't just for pals and fun. Lots of serious business gets done through iChat, both as an instant communication tool and as a way to share files.

You can only send one file at a time through iChat, so if you have more than one, put them all into one folder. Better yet, make an archive, as explained on the previous page.

To copy a file to someone in your Buddy List:

1. Drag the file on top of a buddy name in the list, as shown below. As you drag a file on top of a buddy name, the name area highlights with a bold outline.

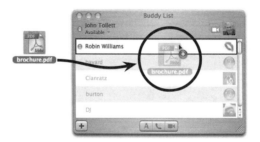

2. An alert message opens on the buddy's computer (below-left).

   The buddy clicks the message to open an "Incoming File Transfer" window that identifies the file being sent.

   The buddy clicks "Save File" (below-right) to accept the transfer. The transferred file is saved to the buddy's Desktop (assuming that's where your Buddy's received files are automatically saved; see the next page).

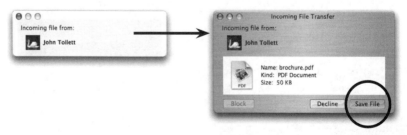

To change the location where iChat file transfers are automatically saved:

1. From the iChat menu, choose "Preferences...."

2. Click the "General" icon in the preferences toolbar.

3. From the pop-up menu shown below, choose the location where you want to save incoming file transfers.

Encrypt iChat messages and files

If both you and your buddy are .Mac members *and* you use .Mac buddy names, you can make sure your file transfers, video chats, audio chats, and text messages are **secure** when you use iChat.

To turn on encryption:

1. From the iChat menu, choose "Preferences...."

2. Click the "Accounts" icon in the toolbar.

3. In the "Accounts" list, choose the .Mac account you want to secure.

4. Click the "Security" tab.

5. Click the "Enable" button.

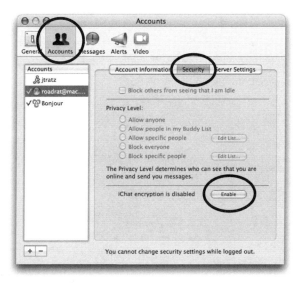

If both parties enable iChat encryption, all communication is sent securely through the .Mac servers.

Bonjour File Sharing

iChat includes a very cool component called **Bonjour.** While iChat requires the Internet to connect users, *Bonjour uses your local network.* Bonjour detects other computers on the network that use Mac OS X and automatically connects to them when iChat is open. This is really handy for quickly transferring files across the room or to an associate who works in another department.

Bonjour file sharing works exactly like the iChat file sharing described on the previous pages:

1. Open iChat.

2. From the Window menu, choose "Bonjour."

3. Drag a file (or a folder of files) on top of a name in the list (as shown below).

The same alert message and Incoming File Transfer window shown on the previous pages appear so the recipient can accept or decline the file being sent.

In Bonjour, drag a file to someone who shows upon the local network

The recipient receives an alert and clicks the alert box to open . . .

. . . the "Incoming File Transfer" window.

.Mac iDisk File Sharing

When you have a .Mac membership, you're assigned a generous amount of data storage space on Apple's computers. The .Mac personal storage is called your **iDisk.** It provides storage for data backups as well as for all sorts of files you can create with .Mac HomePage and iWeb. More to the point, you can place files in your iDisk's "Public" folder for others to access.

For lots more details about using your iDisk, including how to password-protect it, please see Chapter 4, pages 59–64.

To open your iDisk, from the Go menu, choose "iDisk," then choose "My iDisk," as shown below-left. When your iDisk is mounted, an iDisk icon appears on your Desktop, bearing the name of your .Mac membership.

Or if you see an iDisk icon in your Finder window Sidebar, as shown below-right, just single-click on it and your iDisk folders will appear.

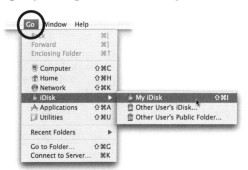

dearrobin

This icon on your Desktop represents an iDisk. Double-click it to open its window.

Upload files to your iDisk "Public" folder

Using one of the three methods above, open the iDisk window to see its folders, including a folder named "Public." *Remember, you're looking at files that are on Apple's servers.* Open another Finder window on your hard disk (press Command N); drag files you want to share *from* your hard disk Finder window *into* the Public iDisk folder. Once they're in your iDisk Public folder, anyone to whom you've given your .Mac user name can download them.

Download files from a .Mac member's Public folder

To download files from someone else's iDisk "Public" folder, all you need is the .Mac user name. (Also see the following four pages for another option.)

1. From the Go menu (shown above), choose "iDisk," then choose "Other User's Public Folder…."

2. Enter a member's account name in the "Member name" field, then click "Connect."

3. The member's iDisk Public folder mounts on your Desktop.

4. Drag files from their Public folder to your own Desktop.

File Sharing with HomePage

A .Mac account includes a feature called HomePage—customizable web page templates that let you quickly and easily create different kinds of web pages to display photo albums, newsletters, etc.

HomePage provides certain templates specifically for sharing files. This type of page is often referred to as an FTP (File Transfer Protocol) site. An FTP site lets you upload files to a web address so anyone on the Internet can download the files. This is a great way to share files with PC users.

You can add password protection to the page if you want to limit access to certain people.

It's simple. Just log in to your .Mac account, create a file sharing page, then upload the files you want to share. Send the web address to whoever needs access to the files. Since .Mac is web-based, you can even create a file sharing site while you're on the go.

The address of all your HomePages will be **homepage.mac.com/yourMacname.**

Two kinds of file sharing pages

HomePage offers two different ways to share files with its special file sharing templates. Before you start to build a page, it's a good idea to know how they are different so you'll know which one to choose.

Remember, it's best to archive files that you upload for sharing; see page 177. If you plan to share a whole folder, you will have to archive it because you can't upload a plain folder, only individual files (an archive is considered an individual file).

My Downloads
(Archival)

▾ **My Downloads.** With this template, you must first put the files you want to share into one of these folders on your iDisk: Movies, Pictures, Public, Sites, or Music. Then you can choose individual files from any of these folders to share on this FTP page.

> **To put files in your iDisk folders:** Open your iDisk (see the previous page or pages 59–64 for details). Drag files from your hard disk and drop them into the appropriate folders on your iDisk.

iDisk Public Folder
(Magenta)

▾ **iDisk Public Folder.** With this template, *every file* you put in your Public iDisk folder will automatically appear on this FTP page. You never have to open HomePage to add or remove files—just drag files in or out of your iDisk Public folder on your Mac (see the previous page).

Create a page for sharing your files

Remember, if you plan to use the "My Downloads" template, first upload the files that are to be shared to the appropriate folder on your iDisk (see the opposite page). You can add additional files later, if necessary.

1. Go to **Mac.com.** Click "HomePage" in the navigation bar (shown below). Log in with your .Mac name and password.

2. If you've never created a HomePage before, you'll see a window similar to the one on the left, below.

   If you have already created a HomePage or two, you'll see the **site management page,** as shown on the right, below.

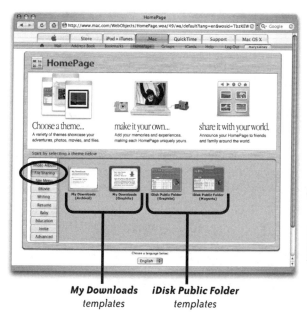

My Downloads   **iDisk Public Folder**
templates   templates

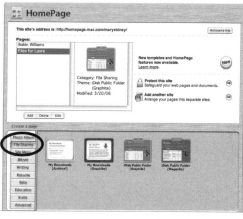

Your **site management page** *might look a little different from this one, depending on what you have already created and what is selected.*

3. Click the "File Sharing" tab, circled in both illustrations above.

4. Choose one of the File Sharing templates shown as thumbnails; see the opposite page for an explanation of the important difference between the two, "My Downloads" and "iDisk Public Folder."

   If you chose **My Downloads,** continue with Step 5a.

   If you chose **iDisk Public Folder,** skip to Step 5b.   *— continued*

5a. Below is an example of the file sharing template called **My Downloads.** Select the existing text and replace it with your own. If you don't replace it or at least delete it, the text you see on the template will appear on the finished web page.

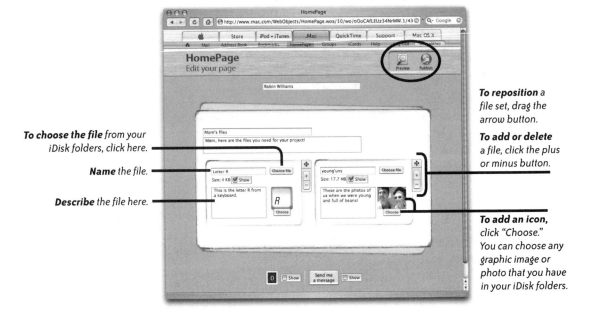

To reposition a file set, drag the arrow button.

To add or delete a file, click the plus or minus button.

To choose the file from your iDisk folders, click here.

Name the file.

Describe the file here.

To add an icon, click "Choose." You can choose any graphic image or photo that you have in your iDisk folders.

6a. Click "Preview" in the top-right corner to see how the page will look when it's published on the web. **To make changes,** click the "Edit" button on the Preview page.

7a. When you're satisfied with how the page looks, click "Publish" (upper-right). You'll get an announcement page with the web address.

To edit your page after you've published it, use the site management window, as shown on page 186.

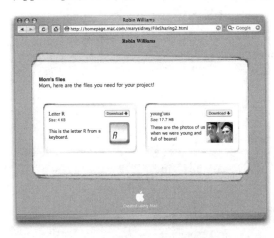

5b. Below is an example of the file sharing template called **iDisk Public Folder.** Select the existing text and replace it with your own. If you don't replace it or at least delete it, the text you see on the template will appear on the finished web page.

If you have files in your Public iDisk folder already, they will appear here as soon as you create the template.

To add more files, just drag them into the Public folder of your iDisk, on your Mac. See pages 59–64 for details about your iDisk.

To remove files, delete them from your Public folder on your iDisk; this page will automatically delete the same files.

6b. Click "Preview" in the top-right corner to see how the page will look when it's published on the web. **To make changes,** click the "Edit" button on the Preview page.

7b. When you're satisfied with how the page looks, click "Publish" (upper-right). You'll get an announcement page with the web address.

To edit your page after you've published it, use the site management window, as shown on the next page.

Visitors can click the "Preview" button to see image files before they download.

Edit your file sharing page

You can edit your file sharing page at any time. After you've published at least one HomePage, you will automatically arrive at the site management page when you click the HomePage button in the navigation bar. Here you can:

- ▼ **Rearrange the order of pages.** In the "Pages" list, drag names up or down to rearrange the order in which their link names appear on your HomePage site.

- ▼ **Change the default page.** Whichever page name is at the top of the list is the one visitors will see first when they go to the site.

- ▼ **Edit a published page.** Select its name in the "Pages" list, then click the "Edit" button just below the list.

- ▼ **Delete a published page.** Select its name in the "Pages" list, then click the "Delete" button just below the list.

- ▼ **Add a new page.** Click the "Add" button. Choose a template. A link to this new page will be placed at the top of every existing page.

- ▼ **Add a password to a page.** Select the page name in the list, then click the arrow button to the right of "Protect this site." Visitors to the page will have to enter that password before they can view the page.

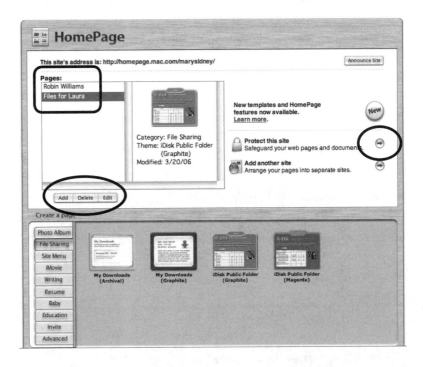

AirPort Extreme and AirPort Express

You can share files using a regular Wi-Fi local network, such as one created with an AirPort Extreme Base Station or an AirPort Express Base Station (see pages 169–171).

When you're within range of a Wi-Fi network, your laptop automatically detects the network and shows it in the AirPort status menu (below-left). Wireless networks also appear in the "Network" pop-up menu in Internet Connect (below-right; Internet Connect is in your Applications folder). **To join any Wi-Fi network detected,** select the network name from either of these two menus.

After you join the Wi-Fi network, make sure "Personal File Sharing" is turned on in Sharing preferences (page 155). Mac OS X users can share files using Bonjour (page 180) or through the local network (pages 192–193).

AirPort Status menu

Internet Connect window

The AirPort status menu bar shows any Wi-Fi networks that are available.

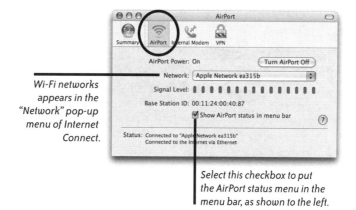

Wi-Fi networks appears in the "Network" pop-up menu of Internet Connect.

Select this checkbox to put the AirPort status menu in the menu bar, as shown to the left.

Create a Computer-to-Computer Network

A computer-to-computer network is sometimes referred to as an *ad hoc* or *peer-to-peer* network.

You may find yourself in a situation where you want to share files with another Mac laptop, but you don't have access to the Internet, a network, or a cable (Ethernet or FireWire) to connect the two. If both Macs have Wi-Fi cards installed, you can create a computer-to-computer wireless network and share files. *This network is not dependent on having an Internet connection available.*

1. Make sure that the two or more Mac laptops you want to connect have Wi-Fi cards (such as AirPort Extreme) installed, and that the distance between them is within Wi-Fi's limited range (realistically, about 100 to 150 feet).

2. From the AirPort status menu (below-left), choose "Create Network...."

   Or open Internet Connect (it's in your Applications folder). Click the "AirPort" icon in the toolbar. From the "Network" pop-up menu (as called out on the previous page), choose "Create Network."

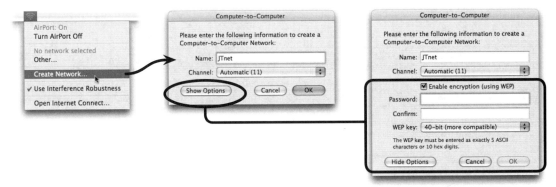

Follow the password requirements shown beneath the "WEP key" menu.

The requirements are different for 40-bit and for 128-bit WEP encryption.

3. In the "Computer-to-Computer" window (above-middle):

   Name the new network.

   Choose a **Channel.** If an existing wireless network is on the same channel, choose a number as far as possible from the existing number.

   To add security, click "Show Options." The window expands to show the WEP (Wired Equivalent Privacy) encryption options (above-right). See Step 4.

4. Click the "Enable encryption" checkbox.

   From the "WEP key" pop-up menu, choose "40-bit" or "128-bit" encryption.

   Type a password in the "Password" field, then retype it in the "Confirm" field.

   Click OK.

5. Select the new computer-to-computer network in the AirPort status menu or from Internet Connect; see Step 2.

To share files, turn on Bonjour on both Macs (see page 180). Bonjour automatically detects other computers on the network. Drag files to a computer name in the Bonjour list, as shown on page 180.

To mount the other computer on your Desktop and access the enitre hard disk (or whatever folders they have chosen to share):

1. Open a Finder window.

2. Choose "Network" in the Sidebar.

3. Double-click a name in the list.

4. If you log on as a **Guest,** you'll have access to the other Mac's Public folder. You can put files in the "Drop Box" folder that's inside their Public folder.

   If you know the **password,** you may have access to the entire hard disk. You need to enter the name and password of the computer you're connecting to.

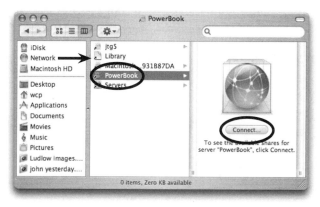

Share Using Ethernet or FireWire Cables

If the computer you want to share files with doesn't have a wireless card installed, you can easily connect the two computers with an Ethernet or FireWire cable.

FireWire cables have different connecters on the ends (4-pin, 6-pin, or 9-pin). Make sure you have the appropriate cable!

Ethernet   6-pin FireWire

1. Connect the two Macs together with an Ethernet or a FireWire cable.

2. In Network preferences, choose "Network Port Configurations" from the "Show" menu. Make sure the Ethernet or FireWire port configuration is checked on (page 176).

3. Click the "Apply Now" button after making changes.

4. In Sharing preferences, make sure "Personal File Sharing" is turned on (see page 176). You can close the preferences window.

5. In your Finder window Sidebar, click the Network icon to mount the connected computer (pages 193–194).

6. Double-click the name of the computer you want to connect to. Enter the name and password for the *other* computer.

7. An icon for the other computer appears on your Desktop. Double-click to open it and drag the folders or files you need to your Desktop.

To unmount the other computer, drag its icon to the Trash.

Use Target Disk Mode

Another method for connecting two Macs so you can share files is with a FireWire cable and "Target Disk Mode." This method is meant as a temporary network and is especially helpful when one computer won't start up and you need to access the files on it.

> The computer whose hard disk you want to see is the **target** computer. *You won't be able to use the target computer during this process.*
>
> The computer that you're using to *see* the other computer is the **host** computer.

1. Connect two computers with FireWire and unplug all other FireWire devices.

2. If using a laptop as the **target** computer, plug in its AC adapter.

3. Turn off the **target** computer. Leave the **host** computer turned on.

4. Start up the **target** computer and immediately hold down the **T key** on its keyboard. Continue holding it down until a FireWire icon appears on its screen.

   Or in System Preferences on the **target** computer, you can choose Startup Disk, then click "Target Disk Mode." Restart the target computer and it will start up in Target Disk Mode. This is useful if you only have one keyboard between the two Macs.

5. An icon of the **target** computer's hard disk appears on the **host** computer's Desktop.

   Double-click its icon to see the **target** computer's contents.

   Drag the files and folders you need to the **host's** Desktop.

6. When you've finished copying files, drag the **target** computer's icon to the Trash to unmount it.

7. Turn off the **target** computer and unplug the FireWire cable.

This is the FireWire icon.

Connect through the Network Icon

If you are on a local network, all of the other computers on the network are found through the "Network" icon in the Sidebar, as shown below. You can easily share files with anyone on this network.

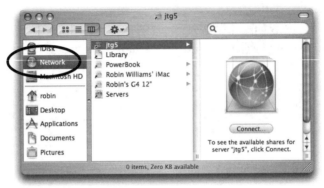

Here you can see all of the other computers that are on this same network. You can access these Macs to share files.

To connect to another Mac on the local network:

1. All Macs that want to connect and share files must have "Personal File Sharing" turned on in the Sharing preferences (see page 176).

2. Open a Finder window, as shown above. Single-click on the "Network" icon in the Sidebar.

   If the Network icon is not in the Sidebar, you can put it there: Go to the Finder menu and choose "Preferences...." Click the "Sidebar" icon in the toolbar. Make sure there is a checkmark next to "Network."

3. You'll see a list of Macs (and PCs) that are connected on this network.

   No matter which view your window is in, you can double-click the name of the computer to which you want to connect.

4. A "Connect to Server" window opens (shown at the top of the next page).

   ▾ **Guest.** If you don't have admin privileges (meaning you don't have the administrator name and password for the other Mac), sign in as a "Guest." Guest access is limited to the "Public" folder, which is in the user's Home folder. The Guest can put files in her Drop Box folder to share, which is inside the Public folder.

   ▾ **Registered User.** If you know the admin name and password of the *other* computer, check this button.

5. If you want to log in as "Guest," choose that button and click

"Connect." You'll have limited access to the other Mac, as explained on the previous page.

If you want to log in as "Registered User," enter the name and password *for the other computer!* I know this window appears and has *your* name in the "Name" field, but it's misleading—it does not want *your* name and password! It wants the name and password for the *other* Mac that you want to connect to. You can use either the long name or the short name.

6. Click the "Connect" button. In the window that opens, shown below, select a "volume" to mount (assuming you entered the name and password for this Mac). Partitions and connected hard disks are shown as volumes in the list. Click OK.

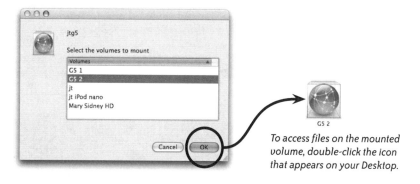

To access files on the mounted volume, double-click the icon that appears on your Desktop.

Tip: Keep a mounted volume accessible by **minimizing** it to the Dock— while its window is open, click the yellow button in the top-left corner.

To re-open the volume's window, just click its icon in the Dock (below).

7. A volume icon of the selected computer appears on your Desktop, as shown above. Double-click it to open a Finder window and access files on that computer.

Connect through the Go Menu

You won't see the Go menu unless you're at the Finder/Desktop, of course!

The Go menu is handy when you know the name and password of an FTP site where you can share files while on your travels. We were able to upload chapters of this book to the Peachpit server while in another country.

To connect to another server, such as an FTP site:

1. From the Go menu, choose "Connect to Server...."

2. In the "Connect to Server" window (below), enter the FTP address you were given. Click "Connect."

If you plan to use this FTP address again, click the + button to add it to your list of "Favorite Servers."

3. Enter the user name and password for the FTP site. Click OK.

ppitt.pearsonEDU.com

This icon appears on your Desktop.

To open *the site window, double-click this icon.*

To disconnect, *drag this icon to the Trash.*

To reconnect *quickly and easily, make an alias of this icon.*

4. The FTP site window appears on your Desktop, as shown below. You can drag files into and out of it.

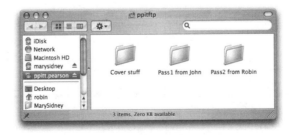

Extra
Road Warrior Tips

The previous chapters cover a great deal of technical information about using a Mac laptop to get connected and stay in touch. Most of the information is fairly easy and very useful to any casual laptop user who needs to be mobile.

This chapter contains lots of tips related to being mobile that

Robin finds an open Wi-Fi network in Mexico.

didn't make it into the other chapters. Some of the information included here is not strictly Mac-related, but we've found it to be useful for the Road Warrior lifestyle, and there might be one or two tidbits here that alone justifies reading this book.

The first of our "extra" Road Warrior tips is (tah-daaah!) the availability of our *Macs On The Go* blog (**web.mac.com/roadrat**). You can check this site regularly, or you can *subscribe* to it and automatically be notified when a new entry is added.

The blog features mobility tips, stories, and photos of getting connected in different places— such as the Wi-Fi network Robin found in Mexico which resulted in a scolding by the nice owner of the wireless network. But not before we checked our mail. Bwahahaha!

We hope to make the blog a friendly, entertaining, and useful space. Visit the site to learn how you can submit your own useful stories, tips, or fun photos.

Troubleshooting

Sometimes bad things happen to good people. Put another way, sometimes computer problems even happen to Mac users. The problems might include not being able to start the computer, or just strange behavior once the computer starts up. The following tips can help keep you digitally sound when your laptop gets goofy.

The Safe Boot procedure

Strange laptop behavior can sometimes be fixed with a simple procedure called a **Safe Boot.**

To run your laptop through a Safe Boot:

1. Turn off the computer.
2. Press the Power button, then immediately after you hear the startup tone, press and hold the Shift key. You can let go of the Shift key when the Apple logo appears on the screen.

When you're in this "Safe Mode," only the files and extensions required to run the computer are loaded. Safe Boot checks and repairs the directory of your hard drive. You can use your computer while in Safe Mode, but some functions may not be available, so it's best to restart before you do any work. This procedure is the same as using the "Repair Disk" command in Disk Utility.

To leave Safe Mode, restart as you normally do. Safe Boot is a good thing to do every so often as maintenance and prevention.

Forced restart

If your laptop is a mess and won't shut down or restart, hold down both the Command and Control keys and press the Power button to force a restart.

Repair disk permissions

Many of the things that you install on your computer create "receipt" files that contain permissions of various kinds. Occasionally these permission files get corrupted, or something happens to them that starts confusing the operating system. As a result, your computer might act strangely and unpredictably. You can often put things back in order with a simple procedure called "Repair Disk Permissions," found in Disk Utility.

To repair disk permissions:

1. Open Disk Utility. You'll find it in the Utilities folder, which is located in the Applications folder.

The Disk Utility icon.

2. In the Disk Utility window, shown below, select your startup hard drive from the list of drives in the left column.

3. Click the "First Aid" tab to show the First Aid pane.

4. Click the "Repair Disk Permissions" button.

   The scrolling text box fills with commands being executed. When Disk Utility is finished, the text box displays the message "Permissions repair complete."

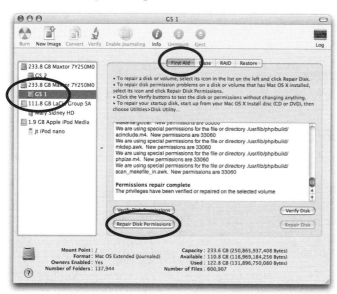

5. Quit Disk Utility and restart the computer.

Reset the Power Manager

The Power Manager is a computer chip inside the laptop. Settings can get confused, causing all sorts of problems such as not waking from sleep or refusing to charge the battery. Resetting the Power Manager returns the hardware to default settings and forces a shut down.

The reset procedure varies for different laptop models. For instance, **to reset a MacBook Pro:**

1. Turn off the computer.
2. Disconnect the AC Adapter and remove the battery.
3. Press and hold the Power button for five seconds.
4. Reconnect the AC Adapter and replace the battery.
5. Restart the laptop.

For other, older models, you might have to remove the keyboard and press a Power Manager reset button. **To find the procedure for your laptop model,** go to **Apple.com,** click the "Support" tab, then type "reset power manager" in the Search field.

Pack a disc of repair utilities

Mac consultants who fix Mac problems for a living usually keep a couple of disk repair utilities in their bag. You can buy the same stuff and carry it with you. Two of the most popular utilities are Alsoft's DiskWarrior (**Alsoft.com**) and Micromat's TechTool Pro (**Micromat.com**).

Pack a system startup disc

When your laptop refuses to start up, insert the Mac OS X startup disc (the one that came bundled with your laptop) in the CD/DVD drive. Press the Power button, then immediately hold down the C key on the keyboard until the computer begins its startup procedure.

Holding down the C key forces the laptop to boot from the disc. Let go of the C key when the graphics appear on the screen.

Do whatever troubleshooting techniques you know how to do, or transfer your important files to another computer (see Chapter 10) just in case your Mac is on its way down.

To restart your laptop from its internal operating system, restart from the Apple menu and hold down the mouse button or the trackpad button (the clicking thing across the bottom of the trackpad) until the CD pops out.

Foreign Language Translation

if you need a simple language translation while on the go, use your Translation widget. **If it's not in your Dashboard already,** you can put it there: Click the Dashboard icon in the Dock, then click the plus symbol in the bottom corner of your screen to show all of your widgets. Click the "Translation" widget to put it on your Dashboard.

Choose the language you want to translate from and the language you want to translate into. Type a word or phrase in English to see it in the selected language. The translations are sometimes inaccurate, so be careful!

The Translation widget as it appears in the Widget Dock.

Another free translation solution is provided by Google. On Google's home page, click the "more" link. On the page that opens, click "translate." Or go straight to **Google.com/language_tools**.

In the "Language Tools" window that opens, type the word or phrase you need translated (shown below-left), then from the pop-up menu choose the language you want to use for the translation.

Google's translation tool.

AltaVista offers a similar translation tool powered by Babel Fish. Look for it at ***world.AltaVista.com.***

Convert Foreign Measurements

When you travel in other countries, their different measurements of distances, quantities, and currency can be confusing. You can download free widgets that convert all types of units used in up to sixty countries around the world, including currency converters that automatically update the currency exchange rates daily.

This is the Easy Currency widget as it appears in the Widget Dock. Click to open it.

The Unit Converter comes with your Mac. It includes a currency converter.

If you don't have the right widget installed, but you do have an Internet connection, you can use Google's built in calculator/converter. In the Search field of **Google.com,** type something like "convert 86 kilometers to miles." Click the "Google Search" button below the search field. The top of the results page (below) shows the calculation.

To convert currency in Google, type something like "convert 4,000 British pounds to US dollars." It's quite amazing.

Search the Internet for "currency converter" to find other free converters online, such as **XE.com.ucc** and **X-Rates.com/calculator.html.** Search the web for "unit converter" to find free online tools that convert all types of units and measurements, such as **DigitalDutch.com/unitconverter.**

Maps on the Go

When you travel to unfamiliar places, good maps make the journey more fun and less stressful. Instead of stuffing your carry-on bag full of unwieldy, folding maps, let your laptop provide the best maps in the world. You can buy map CDs or DVDs for many different countries. But there are also plenty of free map resources on the Internet that you'll love. The following are our favorites.

Google maps

Go to **Google.com** and type a city name in the Search field, then click the "Google Search" button (below-left). The search results page (below-right) includes a "Map of" link near the top of the results list. Click the "Map of" link to show the Google map (bottom).

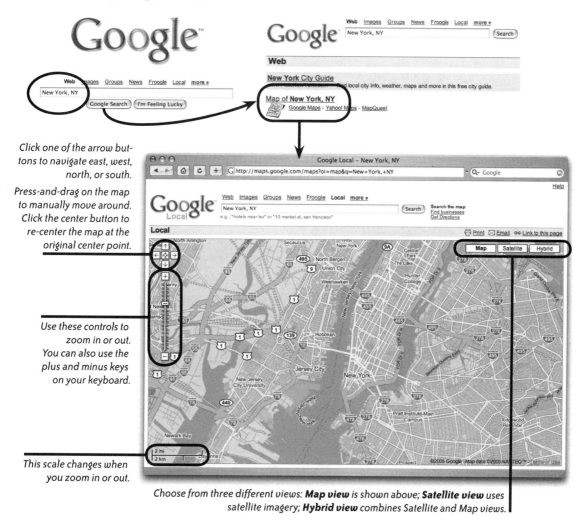

Click one of the arrow buttons to navigate east, west, north, or south.

Press-and-drag on the map to manually move around. Click the center button to re-center the map at the original center point.

Use these controls to zoom in or out. You can also use the plus and minus keys on your keyboard.

This scale changes when you zoom in or out.

*Choose from three different views: **Map view** is shown above; **Satellite view** uses satellite imagery; **Hybrid view** combines Satellite and Map views.*

Find a business (or residence)

Type the name of a business and the town or zip code into the Google Search field. You can type an address, a business name, or something generic like "pizza restaurants" or "emergency medical care." The search results are listed in the left column. If you want to start a new search for a business in another city, just type something like "pizza in Chicago," or "seafood in Morgan City, Louisiana."

Click one of the search results in the left column to highlight it in the map area with an information balloon (shown below).

In addition to entering a search in a single field, you can click "Find businesses" (located to the right of the "Search" button) to show two search fields, labeled "What" and "Where." This can help to narrow down your results.

Find businesses
(or residential addresses).

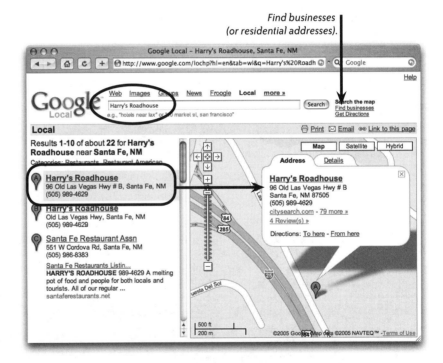

Get driving directions

Google can give you driving directions between two address or even between two cities.

Click the "Get Directions" link (next to the "Search" button). The written directions show in the left column, and the route is marked with a bold line in the map area. Click one of the steps in the list of directions to show a close-up of that section of the route in a bubble balloon (shown below).

To send this map to a friend, click "Email" (shown circled, in the top-right corner of the map area). A new message window opens in your Mail program and a link straight to this map, including the directions, is in the message. When your friend clicks the link, the map page opens in her browser.

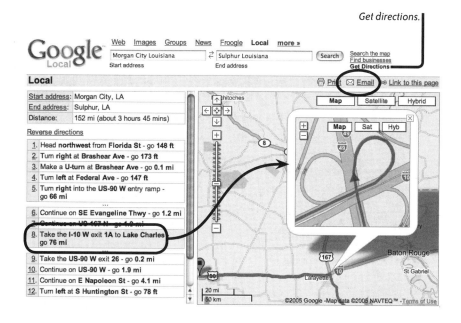

Google Earth

Google Earth is a free satellite map application that you can download from **Google.com.** At Google, click the "more" link, then click the "Earth" link in the "Google Tools" section to download it.

Fly To!

In Google Earth you can "Fly To" anywhere on the planet—click the "Fly To" tab, circled below. In this example, I flew to London: I typed "London" in the text field, then clicked the search button (the magnifying glass).

Google Earth puts various types of information on separate layers, such as Roads, Borders, Buildings, etc. These layers are turned on or off with checkboxes in several places: the "Places" list and the "Layers" list in the left column, and the checkboxes shown below the map area.

Double-click an item in the "Places" list to fly there and see the item in the map view.

Click these checkboxes to show lodging and dining locations.

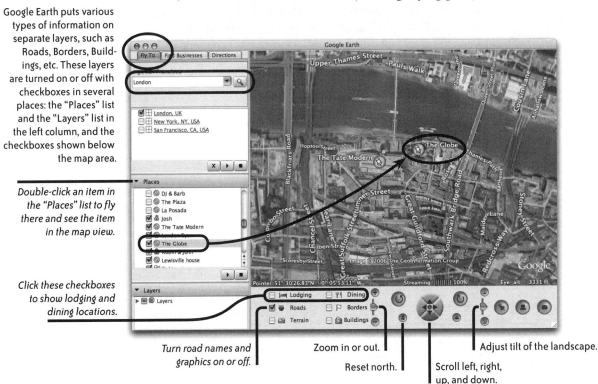

Turn road names and graphics on or off.

Zoom in or out.

Reset north.

Adjust tilt of the landscape.

Scroll left, right, up, and down.

Add a placemark

Placemarks make it easy to find favorite locations. When you placemark a location, it's added to the list of places in the left column. At any time you can double-click a placemark and fly to that location.

1. Click the "Fly To" tab, type an address in the text field, then click the search button (the magnifying glass).

2. When Google Earth finds a specific address for you, a placemark is *automatically* placed on the map at the location you specified.

Sometimes the location of a placemark icon isn't totally accurate. **To move or rename a placemark,** Control-click on it. From the contextual menu that pops up, choose "Edit...," then drag the icon exactly where you want it. In the "Edit Placemark" window that opens (below), change the name if you like, then click OK.

Click here to choose from a variety of different icons to use for the placemark.

3. **To manually placemark a location** that you visually found by scrolling around in the map, click the placemark button in the lower-right corner of the window (shown on the right). A pushpin icon appears on the map. Drag the pushpin icon to the location you want to mark.

The Placemark button.

4. **Zoom in** to see photographic details of the area. Use the zoom control slider located below the map. You can also zoom in or out with the plus and minus keys on your keyboard, or use the scroll wheel on your mouse, if it has one.

Find a business

Click the "Find Businesses" tab (in the top-left corner of the Google Earth window) to locate a business address or even a residential address. In the "What" text field, type something like "Starbucks" (because there's a good chance that Starbucks will have a Wi-Fi connection you can use). In the "Where" text field, use the default "Current view" (unless you want to search for a location in another city). In addition to searching for a specific business name or street address, you can type generic categories into the search field, such as "public library," or "doggie daycare."

Get directions

Click the "Directions" tab to get written and visual directions from one location to another. This works much like the "Get Directions" feature of online Google Local maps (shown on page 203). Instead of showing a close-up in a bubble balloon when you click on a route section in the list of directions, Google Earth animates the route from the current location to the next location in the route.

Show buildings

Ordinary maps show streets and roads, but they aren't very good at giving you a real sense of what a city or a neighborhood looks like. Google satellite photography can help familiarize you with new environments so it's easier to get around. Another visual aid that's available for many major U.S. cities is the Buildings layer. This layer shows buildings rendered in 3D, as shown below. This 3D layer can add a sense of familiarity when you're ready to explore an unfamiliar city.

To use the Buildings layer:

1. Below the map area, click the "Buildings" checkbox to show a gray overlay of building shapes.

2. Move the tilt slider down to change the perspective and show buildings in 3D.

3. Click the Rotate arrows to rotate the 3D view. Use the zoom control to zoom in or out of the image.

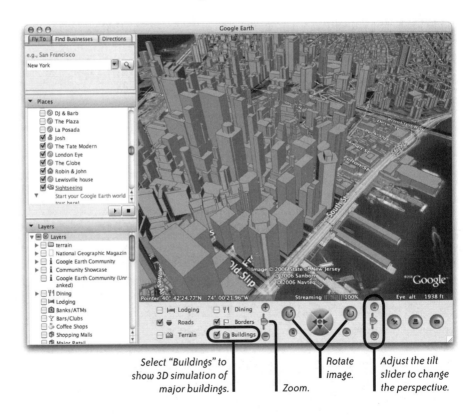

Select "Buildings" to show 3D simulation of major buildings.

Zoom.

Rotate image.

Adjust the tilt slider to change the perspective.

Find the latitude and longitude of a location

Road Warriors who travel with a GPS device will love Google Earth. Wherever you position your cursor on a Google Earth map, the latitude and longitude of that position is displayed in the map's status bar (circled below).

To find the latitude and longitude of a placemark: Select any placemark that appears in the "Places" list (located in the left column) or in the map area to see its latitude and longitude.

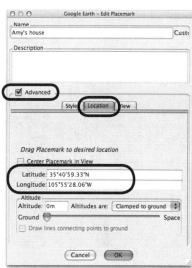

1. From the Edit menu, choose "Properties…" to open the "Edit Placemark" window (on the right).

   Or Control-click on a placemark and choose "Edit…" from the contextual pop-up menu.

2. Click the "Advanced" checkbox to show the Advanced pane settings.

3. Click the "Location" tab to see the latitude and longitude settings of the selected placemark (circled on the right).

Before you leave on a trip, use Google Earth to find locations you want to visit (Internet cafes, hotels, restaurants, museums, an associate's office, etc) and jot down their latitude and longitude settings. Enter the information into your GPS device as waypoints. You can then use your GPS to find those waypoints on your trip.

When you travel, mark locations of interest as waypoints with your GPS device. Later you can enter the latitude and longitude settings of the waypoints into Google Earth to create placemarks, as explained below.

To create a placemark using a known latitude and longitude:

1. From the Add menu, choose "Placemark."

2. In the "Edit Placemark" window that opens (above-right), enter the latitude and longitude of the location you want to add as a placemark.

3. Enter a name for the placemark in the "Name" field at the top.

4. Click OK.

Fly to a specific latitude and longitude

If you know the latitude and longitude of a location, you can "Fly To" it, then create a placemark for it. You'll find the latitude and longitude of almost any town or city at web sites such as **Astro.com, Lat-Long.com,** and **Geocoder.us.**

Click the "Fly To" tab, type the latitude and longitude information in the text field, then click the search button (the magnifying glass). The map area zooms to the exact location.

Measure distances

Google Earth includes a tool with which you can measure distances in every common unit of measurement—feet, miles, kilometers, etc.

To measure a distance, go to the Tools menu and choose "Measure." In the "Measure" window (below-left), click the "Line" or "Path" tab.

> ▼ **Line method.** This measures the distance between two clicks of your mouse.

> ▼ **Path method.** This creates a complex path—click your way along the map (below-right). The path that your mouse makes is measured.

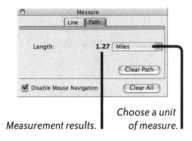

Measurement results.   *Choose a unit of measure.*

The Measure cursor, positioned for the next click.

Use the Terrain layer

Another Google Earth feature that helps provide a sense of familiarity and reality is the **Terrain** layer. Some map areas can show the terrain in 3D, similar to the 3D feature of the Buildings layer (page 206).

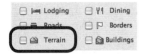

To turn on the Terrain layer, click the "Terrain" checkbox (left) that appears beneath the map area. Use the tilt, zoom, and rotate controls to see the 3D effect (see page 206). For a great example of the Terrain feature, double-click the "Mount Saint Helens" link that Google put in the "Places" list.

MapQuest

MapQuest.com provides extensive online mapping information for the U.S. and Canada; countries outside that area are also covered, but not quite as extensively. **To access foreign maps,** click the "Maps" button on the MapQuest home page, then click the link that says "Outside U.S. & Canada." From the "Country" pop-up menu, choose a country, then enter the name of a city.

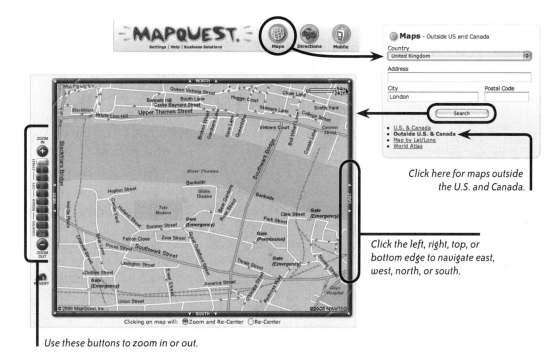

Click here for maps outside the U.S. and Canada.

Click the left, right, top, or bottom edge to navigate east, west, north, or south.

Use these buttons to zoom in or out.

Yahoo maps

Yahoo provides map tools and features that are similar to those available with MapQuest. Go to **Maps.Yahoo.com** to search for a city or a specific address in the U.S. or Canada.

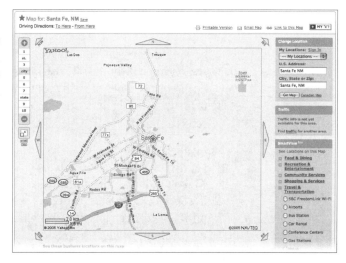

More Chat Clients

Adium   *Fire*

Proteus

iChat is a great app. Love it, love it, love it. But iChat limits your text messaging buddies to those who have .Mac accounts, AIM accounts (AOL), or Jabber accounts. If you need to instant message a friend or business associate who uses another application (such as MSN Messenger, Yahoo! Messenger, or ICQ), what can you do? Simply download a free instant messaging application developed for Mac OS X that's compatible with the other services. Three such clients are Adium (**AdiumX.com**), Fire (**fire.SourceForge.net**), and Proteus (**Defaultware. com/proteus**).

Fax, Voicemail, or Print on the Go

If you need to send or receive a fax while on the go, but don't have access to a phone line (perhaps you're sitting in a bookstore, using their Wi-Fi connection), you can use an online fax service such as **eFax** to send or receive faxes from anywhere you can access email. After you download the eFax software, faxes are sent and received as email attachments.

eFax offers several different plans: **eFaxFree** is free, but has limitations that may not be acceptable, such as having a non-local fax number assigned to you and not being able to send faxes (just receive). **eFaxPlus** has a reasonable monthly fee and limited storage for saved faxes. It includes the ability to send faxes and the use of local or toll-free fax numbers. **eFaxPro** costs a little more and adds the ability to receive voicemails as email attachments and one-year storage of faxes and voicemail. For detailed information, visit **eFax.com.**

eVoice is an online voicemail service. When someone calls your assigned number and leaves a voicemail, it's delivered to your email inbox as a sound file attachment. Sign up for a free account that has limited features or a paid account that includes more features at **eVoice.com.**

If you'd like the same capability as eVoice, but you'd like to use your existing phone number, check out Ovolab Phlink (**www.Ovolab.com/phlink**). Phlink is a package of both software and hardware—a telephone adapter that connects your computer's USB port to an analog phone line. You can set up Phlink to answer your calls at home or office, encode them into small audio files, then send the encoded voice messages to your email account.

Business travelers often need to prepare and print documents while on the go, such as presentation materials that are needed the next morning. **FedEx Kinko's** has an online printing service (FedEx Kinko's Online Document Ordering Service) that lets you upload the documents you need to print. The finished print job can be picked up or delivered to your meeting. Go to **FedEx.com/us** and click the "Office/Print Services" tab.

Wi-Fi VIP Lounges

Some of us spend way too much time in busy, noisy airports waiting for connecting (or delayed) flights. Wouldn't if be nicer to spend that time in a quiet VIP lounge with a wireless connection and big comfortable chairs—maybe even an open bar and refreshments? One way to get that kind of luxury is to fly first class and use the airline's VIP lounge. A much less expensive solution is to buy a **Priority Pass** membership. A Priority Pass gives you access to hundreds of airport VIP lounges around the world. Some lounges provide Wi-Fi phones, fax machines, printers, and even conference rooms. Visit **PriorityPass.com** for membership plans, prices, and detailed information about participating VIP lounges. Believe me, if you often have to spend hours waiting for a flight, an airport lounge membership is a great value.

VoIP

VoIP (Voice over Internet Protocol) technology enables voice calls over the Internet and requires a broadband connection. Two of the most popular VoIP services are described below.

Skype

Skype lets you make free computer-to-computer calls over the Internet to others who have Skype installed on their computers. The basic service allows Skype users to speak to each other for free, or send instant messages or files to each other. You can have conference calls of up to five users at a time. In addition to the basic service, Skype offers SkypeOut and SkypeIn.

The Skype window.

▼ **SkypeOut.** This is an additional paid service that allows Skype users to call an actual telephone number from their computer—a computer-to-phone call.

▼ **SkypeIn.** This paid service lets Skype users receive calls on their computers that originate from traditional phones.

Go to **Skype.com** to download the free software and get detailed information.

Vonage

Vonage is a commercial VoIP service that provides local and long distance calling over the Internet anywhere in the U.S. and Canada for one low price. Some people use this service to replace their traditional phone service. When you sign up, you get a Vonage phone adapter that connects between your phone and your broadband Internet connection. You can take the phone adapter with you and use it in your hotel room or wherever you have a touchtone phone (corded or cordless) and a broadband Internet connection. Several plans are available to fit your needs. Get all of the details at **Vonage.com.**

Bandwidth Speed Testing

It can be comforting (or disappointing) to learn just how fast (or slow) your broadband connection really is. You'll find many sites that provide free speed tests if you search the web for something like "broadband speed test." Two sites are **Speakeasy.net/speedtest** and **MySpeed.VisualWare.com**. Broadband speeds vary depending upon your service and how many people are sharing your connection at any given time.

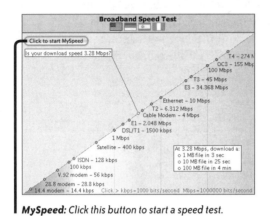

MySpeed: Click this button to start a speed test.

Speakeasy: In the left column, click the server location nearest you to start a speed test.

Spam Filter Options

Even though Mac OS X Mail provides spam and junk mail filters, I still get way too much slimeball stuff in my inbox. If this sounds familiar, check into some of the third-party spam filtering software applications that you can download. Search online for something like "Mac OS X spam filter." Make sure the ones you consider are for use with Mac OS X.

SpamSieve.

Many of these spam filter applications are excellent, but the one that has made digital-life worth living for me is **SpamSieve.** Very few junk mails end up in my inbox, even though I get two or three thousand a day. Instead, they all get sent to a special "Spam" folder that gets emptied in the trash every day.

SpamSieve integrates with the Mac Address Book, so messages from contacts in your Address Book are never accidentally marked as spam. To learn more, visit **C-Command.com/spamsieve**.

Travel Widgets

There's a Dashboard Widget for almost everything. In addition to the widgets that are bundled with Mac OS X, a large and growing collection of other useful widgets can be found on Apple's web site.

To find new widgets to download, go to **Apple.com,** click the "Mac OS X" tab at the top of the page, then click "Widgets" in the navigation bar. Here are a couple of our favorite on-the-go widgets that are included with your Mac.

World Clock

When you travel, you often need to know exactly what time it is where you are, where you're going, or back home. You can open as many World Clock Widgets as you want and show the current time of any location. **To change a World Clock to a different city,** hover your cursor over the clock, then click on the "i" that appears in its bottom-right corner. The clock flips around so you can set a new location. Click "Done" to flip the clock back around.

Flight Tracker

This widget includes flight schedules and tracking for hundreds of airlines around the world. When you need to know where a flight is and when it will arrive at its destination, this will keep you updated.

Enter the airline, departure city, and arrival city, then click "Find Flights."

Select a flight from the column on the right, then click "Track Flight."

You'll see flight information, terminal number, on-time status, and a map of the flight's current location.

More widgets

To find other useful widgets, click the widget icon in the Dock (**A**), then click the "circle +" (**B**) icon to show the Widgets Dock and the "Manage Widgets..." button (**C**). Click the button to open the Widgets Manager window (right). In the window, click "More Widgets..." to browse Apple's Widgets web page.

A   B   C

Checkmark a widget to activate it. A circle-dash to the right of a widget indicates it's from a third-party developer.

Other Mobile Devices

Speaking from personal experience, Road Warriors sometimes become slightly obsessed with collecting gadgets that can enhance their hi-tech and digitally connected lifestyle. All you really need is your laptop, but we'll mention three other mobile devices that you may want to include in your travel bag if you have an urge to crank it up a notch with the Road Warrior thing.

iPod

The iPod is not only the most popular music and video player available, it can also serve as a portable hard disk to backup or transport files.

1. Plug in your iPod to *your* Mac.

2. Open iTunes preferences and choose the "iPod" icon in the toolbar (below-left).

3. Click the "Music" tab, then check "Enable disk use."

4. When you choose "Automatically update all songs and playlists," the contents of your iPod are *replaced* with the iTunes contents of the computer you connect to. You may not want to do this. **To prevent automatic updating of songs and playlists,** choose the option to "Manually manage songs and playlists."

5. Click OK. An iPod icon is displayed on your Desktop (right). Double-click the icon to open it as an iPod window (below-right). Drag folders or files from your computer to the iPod window to copy them to the iPod.

jt iPod nano

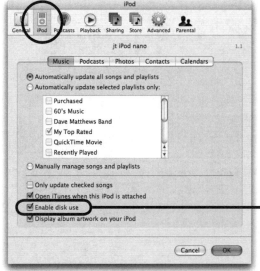

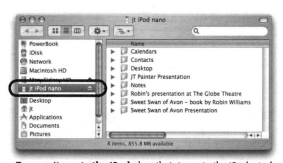

To copy items to the iPod, *drag their icons to the iPod window.*
To copy items back to a computer, *drag them from this window to the Desktop or into any folder or open window.*

Put a check in this checkbox to make your iPod act as a hard disk.

PDA (Personal Digital Assistant) device

A Wi-Fi enabled PDA, such as a Palm handheld device, is handy to have when a laptop is too big to carry around. However, be aware that the built-in browser in some PDAs may not support certain kinds of web pages (such as pages with pop-up windows), which may prevent you from logging in to your .Mac account or into a paid Wi-Fi account at a wireless hotspot.

If you decide to use a Wi-Fi PDA instead of a laptop while on the go, consider buying a portable keyboard to make typing less frustating. Portable keyboards fold to a very small size and communicate with the PDA through a wireless infrared signal.

GPS (Global Positioning System) device

A GPS is not only fun, it's incredibly useful when you're traveling in unfamilar cities and countries. My GPS has kept us from getting lost on deserted New Mexico backroads in the middle of the night, and it helped us find our way back to the hotel after walking around Rome for hours.

In the past, connecting a GPS to a Mac was a challenging experience (if not downright unpleasant). It's not as if you can't connect a GPS to a Mac, it's just not as simple as it should be, some of the best GPS software is not available for Mac OS X, and we don't have space enough here to address all of the issues. However, things have been changing for disenfranchised Mac users lately, and Garmin (one of the leading makers of GPS devices) recently announced that they are adding support for the Mac platform. This is really exciting news for Mac/GPS owners. Soon we'll be able to GPS ourselves silly. Meanwhile, you can get a lot of GPS use out of your Mac with a little help from Google Earth (see pages 207).

Broadband Tuner 1.0

To take full advantage of high speed Internet connections, download and install a small application from **Apple.com/support** called Broadband Tuner 1.0. This application increases the default size of TCP (Transmission Control Protocol) Send and Receive buffers. Larger buffers allow more data to be in transit at once. Mac OS X 10.4 or later is required.

Mobile Broadband Service

EVDO is not Wi-Fi. It's WWAN, Wireless Wide Area Network.

Wouldn't it be great if you could tap into a broadband connection to the Internet that's as mobile as your cell phone? You can—if you subscribe to a mobile broadband service. Verizon provides a wireless broadband technology known as **EVDO,** short for Evolution Data Only or Evolution Data Optimized. Sprint has started rolling out a similar service that they call Wireless High-Speed Data, but their coverage area is not yet as extensive as Verizon's.

When you subscribe to an EVDO service (usually $60–$80 a month), you get broadband access anywhere in your provider's service area. Just as you expect your mobile phone to connect to your phone service from almost anywhere, now you can expect your laptop to jump on the Internet from almost anywhere. You can even connect to the Internet while driving down the highway (if someone else is actually doing the driving), commuting on a train, or sitting in a backpacker tent in the mountains. Hmm, a new reason to go for a hike.

And you don't need to jump through hoops getting your mobile phone to act as a modem. If your laptop has a PC slot, you can buy an EVDO PC card that inserts and connects to your EVDO service. The EDVO PC card acts as receiver and transmitter for the wireless signal. The newest Mac laptops, such as the MacBook Pro, don't include traditional PC slots—instead they have a new, smaller slot called ExpressCard/34. Expect developers to release EVDO Express-Card/34 options very soon.

All Verizon service areas do not necessarily include wireless broadband service. Visit the Verizon site (**VerizonWireless. com**) to see coverage maps of Verizon's wireless broadband service.

One solution for owners of laptops with ExpressCard/34 slots is to buy an EVDO router, which is a separate, small box that can rebroadcast the signal as a Wi-Fi signal. An AirPort-enabled laptop (such as the MacBook Pro with an ExpressCard/34 slot) can receive the rebroadcast signal.

EVDOinfo is an authorized Verizon agent. Visit **EVDOinfo.com** for information and expert Mac EVDO help. You'll find lots of advice, tips, user forums, and service coverage maps. They can help you choose the right EVDO card for your laptop and any other items that you may need, such as a booster antenna or an EVDO router. If you buy an EVDO card and service from EVDOinfo, you'll get free support from the Mac experts there.

This is Verizon's EVDO PC card.

Share your EVDO *or AirPort connection*

When you connect to the Internet wirelessly, either through an EVDO card and paid subscription or through an AirPort card and Wi-Fi connection, you can share that Internet connection with others. For instance, let's say you're traveling with a PowerBook that has an AirPort card installed (or an EVDO card inserted in the PC card slot) and the laptop with which you want to share a connection is AirPort-enabled.

To share your Internet connection, turn on Internet Sharing:

1. Open System Preferences, then choose "Sharing."

2. Click the Internet tab (circled below).

3. From the pop-up menu ("Share your connection from"), choose the name of the card that's providing your current Internet connection.

4. If the other computer has an AirPort card installed, put a checkmark next to "AirPort" in the list of Internet connection ports.

5. Other computers with an AirPort card (or other brands of Wi-Fi cards), can detect the Wi-Fi signal that your laptop is broadcasting and connect to it.

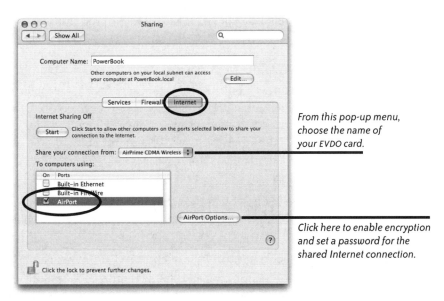

From this pop-up menu, choose the name of your EVDO card.

Click here to enable encryption and set a password for the shared Internet connection.

Acoustic Coupler

Imagine you're driving through a small town in NowhereSpecial. Your mobile phone's service provider is out of range. It's Sunday and nothing is open. You really need to go online so you can send an important message. My oh my, is that a payphone over there? Why not use an acoustic coupler and connect your laptop to the payphone. OK, this is pretty extreme, but someone out there might need it.

An acoustic coupler lets you connect your laptop (if it has a modem) to virtually any telephone—even payphones or hard-wired phones that don't use an RJ-11 cable. An acoustic coupler attaches to the handset of a phone using a Velcro strap. The coupler's RJ-11 cord plugs into the RJ-11 port (the modem port) on your laptop.

When your laptop dials your ISP's number, the modem beep sounds are transferred to the phone handset. This may not work every time, especially on older payphones, but at least it provides a possible connection option, even if you're in another country with a hard-wired phone in your hotel room.

To find an acoustic coupler, go to any of the popular online shopping sites, such as **Froogle.com** or **PriceGrabber.com** and search for "acoustic coupler."

To use an acoustic coupler:

Make sure your Internal Modem is turned on in Network preferences; see pages 26–28.

1. Open Internet Connect. Enter settings to dial your ISP, as explained in Chapter 3. When you enter the ISP phone number, you can avoid having to add coins to a payphone by adding a calling card number in front of the ISP number. Or use an 800 number service, such as the one provided by EarthLink and many other ISPs.

2. Connect the coupler's RJ-11 cord to the modem port on your laptop.

3. Strap the acoustic coupler to the phone's handset, matching the speaker to the phone's mouthpiece and the microphone to the phone's earpiece.

4. Click the "Connect" button in Internet Connect.

   If you have trouble connecting, try dialing manually. From Internet Connect's "Connect" menu, choose "Manual Dial," then use the phone to dial your ISP number.

Remember, the new MacBook Pro laptops don't have internal modems or RJ-11 ports. If you have one of these laptops, you'll need to buy an external modem. Apple sells a small USB modem that's perfect for travel. Go straight to **Apple.com,** or go to **Apple.com** and click the "Store" tab.

Index

portable storage devices, 19
Post Office Protocol, 71
PostScript printers, 30
power adapters, 15–16
PowerBook
  and AirPort cards, 217
  feature summary, 10–11
  Fkey behavior on, 23
  and iSight cameras, 102
  keyboard, 21–22
  vs. other models, 12
  reading digital publications on, 3–4
  and shared Internet connections, 217
Power Manager, 198
power supplies, 15–16
power transformers, 16
PPP options, 36
PPPoE, 30
PPTP, 52
Pre-n products, 165
preferences
  Date & Time, 126–27
  Keyboard & Mouse, 23–24
  Network. *See* Network settings
  Print & Fax, 146
  Security, 151–52
  Sharing, 155, 176, 217
presentations, 2–3, 210
PriceGrabber.com, 19, 218
printing
  documents, 210
  faxing as alternative to, 143–44
  photos, 96
  text chats, 108
Priority options, iCal, 129
Priority Pass membership, 211
Private Browsing feature, Safari, 150, 218
private chat rooms, 107
private networks, 163
Proteus chat client, 210
proximity alarms, wireless, 149
proxy servers, 30, 37
public calendars, 135
Public folder, iDisk, 62, 63, 181, 182

publishing
  blogs, 88–89
  calendars, 132–33
  movies, 94–95
  photo albums, 90–92
  Photocasts, 96–97

Q

Quick Address menu, 75

R

reader software, 3
receipt files, 197
Registered User access, 192, 193
reminders. *See* To Do lists
Repair Disk Permissions, 197
repair utilities, 198
reset procedure, 198
reverse polarity, 162
Right Control key, 24
RJ-11 cables, 13, 147, 218
RJ-45 cables (Ethernet), 14
Road Warrior lifestyle, 195
roaming services, 160
RSS feeds, 2

S

Safari
  bookmarks, 5, 57, 78–79
  Clear History command, 150
  History menu, 150
  Private Browsing feature, 150
Safe Boot procedure, 196
Safe Mode, 196
satellite connections, 164
satellite maps, 204–8
screen savers, 57, 86–87
search feature, iCal, 130–31
Secure Empty Trash feature, 150
Security preferences, 151–52
Security settings, iChat, 113
security systems, laptop, 149